SACRAMENTO

A MINI-HISTORY

by
 Phyllis Zauner

Artist: **Neva Roberts**

P.O. Box 8306   South Lake Tahoe, CA 95731

ZANEL PUBLICATIONS
P. O. Box 1387
Sonoma, CA 95476

Picture Credits

California State Library, pages   1, 2, 5, 6, 7, 11, 12, 14, 16, 20, 22, 23,
24, 27, 31, 33
Sacramento City-County Library, page, 23
Bancroft Library, pages   15,   9, 10
Joseph E. Smith, page 37
Southern Pacific, pages 28, 29

ZANEL publications:

California Gold, Story of the Rush to Riches
Carson City, Capital of Nevada
Lake Tahoe, The Way It Was Then and Now
Sacramento and the California Delta
San Francisco, The Way It Was Then and Now
The Cowboy, An American Legend
Those Legendary Men of the Wild West
Those Spirited Women of the Early West
Virginia City, Its History ... Its Ghosts

Library of Congress Catalog Card Number: LC79-55950
ISBN No. 0-936914-02-5

SUTTER'S FORT: A PRELUDE

"Sutter received us with open arms and in a princely fashion, for he was a man of the most polite address and the most courteous manners, a man who could shine in any society."

The fact that such a courtly gentleman chanced to be playing host in a land then more remote than is now any spot on our whole globe, is one of the remarkable tales of the remarkable early West.

And genial John Sutter, urbane and polished, was one of the West's most remarkable pioneers.

Dapper young Capt. John Sutter, who wandered half around the globe to found an Empire on the Sacramento River

Sutter arrived in Yerba Buena (San Francisco) by way of Fort Vancouver, Oregon Territory, from which port he took passage to the Sandwich Islands (Hawaii), made friends with King Kamehameha, sailed to Sitka, Alaska, and finally made his way to the land of his ambitions — California — where he planned to build an empire he could command as his very own.

That he ever achieved such an ambitious dream is a monumental tribute to an overwhelming personal magnetism.

During the course of his wayward journeys, this affable traveller had acquired, toward his ultimate goal, a large assortment of provisions, tools and agricultural implements, an arsenal of weapons, a cannon or two — and had recruited a crew of followers that numbered, according to his own account, "five white men and eight Kanakas."

It was with this varied assortment of assets that he approached Governor Alvarado, the 30-year-old Mexican then in charge of running California, and requested lands on which to settle in the uninhabited Sacramento Valley.

He couldn't have arrived at a more auspicious time. Governor Alvarado was delighted.

The fact is, he was having a few problems of his own, and in Captain Sutter he saw a savior. Mexico's rule over its northern province of

Alta California was faltering. The Indians were unruly. There was the constant threat of foreign invaders (Russia was already ensconced at Fort Ross). And trappers were beginning to arrive in ever-increasing poaching forays over the Sierras from the United States.

Now here, God bless him, was a man willing to take on the dangers of pacifying the Indians, and representing Mexico in the remote inland region, thus discouraging encroachment of American settlers.

Making Sutter a Mexican citizen was only a formality. He was accorded full permission to explore the rivers and to select and take possession of any location that might please him, with the assurance that after the expiration of one year from settlement his title would be confirmed. He had Alvarado's promise he might command eleven Spanish leagues (76 square miles) of any unoccupied land he found convenient.

And so, with Alvarado's blessing, Sutter set off on what he later called "my exploratory journey to find the mouth of the river Sacramento, for I could find nobody who could give me information, only that they knew that some very large rivers were in the interior."

Before leaving Yerba Buena he arranged for the outfitting of three boats. And on August 1, with three German carpenters, two mechanics, and the eight Hawaiians, he headed off into the labyrinth that is the Delta.

Those who saw him off looked upon his foolhardy project of colonizing California's interior as harebrained, if not downright idiotic.

As for the captive Hawaiians -- since leaving their native tropical island they'd seen Alaska, Monterey, and San Francisco. By now they were seasoned travellers.

The "white" men in the party, however, admitted to moments of queasiness as they set off into a wilderness populated only by Indians and mosquitoes.

> "Well, I tell you, in the early days the Delta was a mosquito and swamp story. There was so many mosquitos they'd close the sun at evening." ...Recollections of an Old Timer.

Recorded Sutter in his diary:

> *It took me eight days before I could find the entrance to Sacramento, as it is very deceiving and very easy to pass by, how it happened to several Officers of the Navy afterwards which refused to take pilot. I fell in with the first Indians which was all armed and painted and looked very hostile, they was about 200 armed Men, as some of them understood a little Spanish I could make a Kind of Treaty with them, and the two which understood Spanish came with me, and made me a little better acquainted with the Country. All the other Indians on the up River hided themselves in th bushes, and on the Mouth of Feather River they runned all away so soon they discovered us. I was examining the Country a little further up with a boat, while the larger crafts let go their Ankers, on my return, all the white Men came to me and asked me, how much longer I intended to travel with them in such a Wilderness.*
>
> *The following Morning I gave Orders to return, and entered in the American River, landed on the 12th Augt. 1839.*

The land Sutter chose was a gently rising knoll well back from both rivers.

The first task was to set up tents, then proceed to the construction of three Hawaiian-style grass huts. Before the winter rains set in, an adobe building had been completed, nearly 40 feet long, which became the nucleus of Sutter's Fort, one of the most famous of all western frontier outposts.

the civilized frontiersman

Notwithstanding his regal manner and an outstanding executive ability as a leader of men, John Sutter came of humble beginnings.

He set out in the business world at Basel, Switzerland as a printer's apprentice, didn't like it, became a draper's clerk, didn't like that, either. His career showed some improvement after he married Anna Dubeld (the day before their son was born) because her mother, a widow, had money and was willing to set her son-in-law up in the dry goods business.

It was in this venture that Sutter first exhibited the serious defect in business management that was to harass him throughout his life. As John Bidwell was to discover years later: "He had peculiar traits, his necessities compelled him to take all he could buy, and he paid all he could pay; but he failed to keep up with his payments, and so he soon found himself immensely — almost hopelessly — involved in debt."

His was an expansive nature. He liked living on a grand scale. He had a taste for lavish entertainment. He couldn't say no to anyone, even those asking for credit.

The consequences were inevitable. When the firm's liabilities exceeded assets three-to-one, and Mama refused to shell out any more, John Sutter packed up his fancy shirts and whatever cash he could lay his hands on, and left the country without saying good-bye to his wife or his four children. He made his way to the New World.

Mrs. John Sutter:
The Girl He Left Behind

And here, in the New World, began the fictionalization of John Sutter — "captain in the Swiss Army, officer in the service of Charles X of France, son of a clergyman." Was there any harm? Since it was his lot to be a fugitive from the past (and stringent Swiss laws), and to build a new image, why not make it one of which he could be proud?

He headed for Missouri and engaged in several trading ventures there and in New Mexico. It was in Santa Fe that he first heard of California and realized, in his self-dramatizing way, that it was his destiny to establish a colony there and be its ruler.

His decision to head west was hastened by the failure of his general store in Missouri.

Again on the run, he worked his way to Oregon ("under a good many dangers and other troubles," he said), and from there canoed to Fort Vancouver, where he hoped to get passage to California.

By now he was totally immersed in his role as Captain Sutter, and completely captivated the commanding officer. Since nothing was sailing for California, he settled for Hawaii, hoping to take passage from there. He carried with him a glowing letter of introduction from Commander Douglas to the King of the Sandwich Islands (Hawaii). Still unable to find passage to California, he spent several months there hobnobbing with leading dignataries. In fact, King Kamehameha urged Capt. Sutter (of the Swiss Army!) to take charge of his military forces.

Impatient at waiting, he sailed to Alaska (where he made friends with a Russian officer, a contact that proved valuable later at Fort Ross), and finally sailed from there to California.

To say Sutter was a fake would be to do him an injustice. Although his credentials weren't honest, he carried in him always the values of a gentleman: persuasiveness, courtly manners, an ever-buoyant nature, irresistible charm, a talent for sparkling conversation, and an ability to see visions of grandness.

THE FORT FLOURISHES

In those early years of westering, few emigrants made their way to California.

The barrier of the Sierra Nevadas was a formidable one; California was Mexican territory, a "foreign" land; and the Oregon Trail, by now well marked, was *the way* to head West.

Withal, Sutter's life in the valley between mountain and shore was not a lonely one. He was busy.

With the help of available Indian labor and an occasional passing American, he constructed his Fort (now familiar), with its 18-foot walls, its headquarters building, and its long line of workshops. He laid a rough road down to an embarcadero on the Sacramento River so he could ship goods to San Francisco. By the following summer he had planted crops and acquired some cattle and horses to graze in the outlands of his 11-league plot of land.

One of Sutter's guests in 1841 was Capt. Wilkes, a government agent. "Sutter is a person of great urbanity of manner and considerable intelligence," Wilkes wrote in his report. "He has even succeeded in winning the goodwill of the Indians, who are now laboring for him building houses and a line of wall to protect him. He treats the Indians kindly, and pays them well for their services in trapping and working for him.

No doubt about it, Sutter showed remarkable success with taming the Indians. He had an understanding of their temperament, and an ability to direct their activities into channels useful to him. He gave them work to do and paid them for that work, usually in clothes or colorful beads and ornaments. He organized them into a military company, with uniforms (which they loved) and taught them a few drill maneuvers. "The Indians were sometimes troublesome," he said, "but on the whole I got along nicely with them."

It didn't always go smoothly, of course. Pilfering was a continuing problem. The Indians saw all around them what they considered great material possessions, and they failed to understand by what laws they were excluded from sharing in this wealth. The frequent booming of the Fort's cannons served as a convincer for a while. They adopted a course of passivity and great kindness, which, unfortunately, lulled Sutter into a sense of security that almost resulted in the destruction of the entire camp. If it hadn't been for the vigilance and instincts of a large bulldog Sutter had brought with him from the Sandwich Islands, history might have ended then and there on the American River.

One dark night a band of Indians took upon themselves the mission of stealing into

Sutter's quarters to assassinate the entire company. This bulldog, concealed in darkness, silently watched the stealthy movements until the foremost Indian was about to attack, then sprang on the ringleader and fastened his teeth into him.

The bulldog proved to be a better convincer than the cannons.

The next day, Sutter, ever kind, made the incident the point for a lecture. "I told them I would forgive them this time but that further attempts would be met with severe punishment." Thereafter he kept a closer watch on their activities.

Sutter had arrived in California with very little money. And in those early months of empire-building, finances continued to plague him. He had a temporary friend, though, in Ygnacio Martinez, a rancher on the Carquinez Strait whom he had met while waiting for his boats to be outfitted at Yerba Buena. Martinez at least gave Sutter a meager start on cattle and horses, and seed for the land. All on credit, of course.

Later, having worn out his welcome with Martinez through failure to pay his bill, he got a second herd from August Sunol, a rancher in present-day San Jose. On credit.

He had a few visitors. In 1841 John Bidwell and a party of thirty came over the Sierras. In 1842 there was no one. In 1843 another party of emigrants braved the Sierras. By 1845 over 200 had come through Sutter's Fort, including Lt. John Fremont, whom Sutter never liked and felt was responsible for the citizen's Bear Flag Revolt.

John Charles Fremont, sometimes called the Pathfinder, was regarded by some to be a "path follower"

"Nearly everybody who came to California," wrote John Bidwell, (who stayed on at the Fort to help Sutter) "made it a point to reach Sutter's Fort. Sutter was one of the most liberal and hospitable of men. Everybody was welcome — one man or a hundred, it was all the same."

a deal with russia

Unexpectedly, Sutter now acquired the entire settlement of Fort Ross, including the horses, cattle and sheep he needed so badly. The Russians, discouraged by depletion of otters and the harshness of the land, and nettled by the Mexicans, sold out all they owned to amiable John Sutter for $30,000. Two thousand down, the rest on credit, payable over the next four years in wheat to Russia.

Diary entry, Sept. 4, 1841: Arrived at Russian Governor on board the schooner Sacramento. Offered me their whole establishment at Bodego and Ross for sale. We dined on board the Helena and closed the bargain for $30,000. Champaigne flowed freely; we drank to the health of the Russian Emperor, and I was toasted as the new owner of Ross and Bodega.

Sutter had an unerring ability as a real estate developer, and an instinct for largescale thinking.

But events were developing in the wings that were to remove John Sutter from center stage. The great dreams he had for turning his Fort and a town called Sutterville (then in the planning stage), into a center of inland commerce, were to be replaced by another dream of another town, promoted by another man.

Sacramento City was, basically, the city of Sam Brannan.

Sam Brannan, Entrepreneur

Sam Brannan was an ambitious man. He was only 31 when he left New York on the ship *Brooklyn*, leading a band of Mormons to what he believed to be the promised land of Zion in the country called California. The distinction of finding Zion, however, was to be reserved for another ambitious Mormon, Brigham Young.

"In any group of men, Brannan was a striking figure," according to a contemporary account, "deep chested, shaggy headed, coarse in manners, bombastic in speech. He dressed in the style of a dandy. With unbounded courage he launched forth with a personal initiative that knew no fear."

In the cargo of the *Brooklyn* he stowed a printing press. Within a fortnight of landing in San Francisco, he set up the press and was printing the city's first newspaper (second in California) — the *California Star*.

He launched into a career as an entrepreneur which soared to great heights and then collasped disastrously. Early on, he parted ways with the Church, for he was hopelessly at loggerheads with Brigham Young over a small technicality — he was collecting tithes and not turning them in.

In the autumn of 1847 Brannan visited Sutter at the Fort and arrangements were made to open up a general store at the Fort, the first of its kind in the Sacramento Valley.

Later, when gold was discovered, another Brannan store was opened, filled with a huge stock which was retailed to the miners at enormous profits. This was the beginning of Brannan's strong influence in building a city at the waterfront. In the end, it turned Sutter's Fort into a has-been outpost.

It was Brannan's destiny to become the richest man in the state.

For a time, everything he touched turned to money. At one time he owned most of the property on Market Street in San Francisco, and one-fifth of the property in Sacramento. He bought saw mills in Nevada. Acquired Calistoga Hot Springs. An unabashed extrovert, Brannan reveled in his wealth. He pursued the actress Lola Montez, issued his own paper currency from a bank he founded, served on the city council and in the state senate. He bought the Odd Fellows a cementary, the fire company an elaborate fire engine. He gave freely, never minding the trouble or expense.

But his great ambition was also his undoing. Some of his land speculations proved unlucky. His wife hit him with a costly divorce. Indians poached on his land. He took to drinking.

His later years didn't have the brilliant shine that his early years promised. But he wrote a fantastic personal chapter of life in California before he died — a broken, semi-alcoholic dreamer.

He was one of the first men in California who truly saw its possibilities.

GOLD FEVER: INCURABLE DISEASE

"Only lunatic asylums can effect a cure of the present ills...at least until hunger drives all the visionary fools from the gold diggins."

...*Army Capt. J. Folsom*

Perhaps no account of the discovery of gold in California could match the poignancy of James Marshall's own recollections.

"One morning in January — it was a clear, cold morning, I shall never forget that morning — as I was taking my usual walk along the race after shutting off the water, my eye was caught with the glimpse of something shining in the bottom of the ditch. There was about a foot of water running then. I reached my hand down and picked it up. It made my heart thump, for I was certain it was gold. The piece was about half the size and of the shape of a pea. Then I saw another piece in the water. After taking it out I sat down and began to think right hard. I thought it was gold, and yet it did not seem to be of the right color. All the gold coin I had seen was of a reddish tinge; this looked more like brass. I recalled to mind all the metals I had ever seen or heard of, but I could find none that resembled this.

"Suddenly the idea flashed across my mind that it might be iron pyrites. I trembled to think of it! This question could soon be determined. Putting one of the pieces on a hard river stone, I took another and commenced hammering it. It was soft, and didn't break. It therefore must be gold, but largely mixed with some other metal, very likely silver, for pure gold, I thought, would certainly have a brighter color."

James Marshall was a taciturn, introverted 37-year-old carpenter who had contracted with Sutter to build a sawmill on the American River, in the foothills above Sacramento. It was while dredging out the tailrace of the mill (the channel that carries water away from the revolving wheel) that Marshall discovered, early on a January morning, gold nuggets in the fine silt that had washed over the rocks.

The discovery by no means precipitated an instant gold rush.

In fact, Marshall waited several days before making a trip to Sacramento to tell Sutter the news. He asked to see the Captain alone in his private quarters. "Marshall asked me if the door was locked, and I replied no, but I shall gladly lock it. I knew he was a very strange man, and I took the whole thing as a whim of his..."

After Sutter had seen the gold specimen, he took out an old encyclopedia to find the test for gold, went to the apothecary shop and got aqua fortis, tested it. It was, indeed, gold.

Excited as he was, it wasn't hard for him to foresee what would happen to his various enterprises once the word got out that there was gold for the picking. The two men agreed to keep the matter quiet until the sawmill was finished and the new flour mill completed.

But as a practical matter, the secret was out. Some of the men working for Marshall were doing some prospecting on their own. More gold was found. The cook's small son gave a few nuggets to a worker who had come up from the Fort, who took it back and tried to use it to buy whiskey.

It wasn't for another month, though, that the first press account appeared in a San Francisco newspaper. Then it was back page news. No one was stirred. Small discoveries had been reported in other regions, now and then, but never had developed to anything big.

Actually, no one cared. California then was sleepy, agricultural, virtually unpopulated.

Aside from the Indians, there weren't more than 2,000 people in the entire territory. Population of San Francisco was 460; at Sacramento and the Fort inhabitants didn't exceed 150. And those were northern California's most sizable communities.

But the rumors kept coming. And the size of the nuggets grew. Finally, in May, Sam Brannan left his store at Sutterville to investigate for himself. What he saw electrified him. He stuffed some nuggets into a quinine bottle, rushed to San Francisco, and rode down Montgomery Street waving the gold and shouting at the top of his booming voice, "Gold! Gold on the American River!"

That did it. Gold fever had finally infected the sleepy little port. Within a week San Francisco was all but deserted. The stampede was on.

> *By boat, by mule and horse, or on foot they went, all eager to reach the mines, fearing the gold would be gone before they could get there. Business houses closed their doors. There was no service in the little church in the plaza and a padlock was on the door of the mayor's office.*
> *...San Francisco Report*

The news spread across the West coast...to Oregon...to Los Angeles...Mexico, Hawaii, Chile. The adult male population decamped in a body for the "diggins", leaving only women and children behind.

The effect on hospitable John Sutter was chaotic.

"The great Rush from San Francisco arrived at the fort, all my friends and acquaintances filled up the houses and the whole fort, I had only a little Indian boy, to make them roasted Ripps etc. as my Cooks had left me like everybody else."

Sam Brannan, however, was doing very well. He had just opened up a new store, convenient to miners.

It was soon discovered that in all of San Francisco there wasn't a single mining pan to be found. Sam Brannan had bought them all up. Originally priced at 20 cents, they were now selling at Brannan's store for a half-ounce to one ounce of gold dust — $8 to $16 each.

John Bidwell was one of the first to take a flyer at mining, and became fabulously wealthy. In 1890 he was the Prohibition Party candidate for Governor, but received only 10,000 votes.

Oddly enough, no one rushed from the East the first summer, even when the newspapers got down to specifics and reported that ten million dollars in gold had been mined (and that's a lot of gold!).

What started the Rush of Forty-Nine was a report sent to President Polk by Col. Mason from San Francisco:

Along the route (to Sutter's Fort) mills were lying idle, fields of wheat were open to cattle and horses, houses vacant, and farms going to waste. At Sutter's there was more life and business. Capt. Sutter had only two mechanics in his employ, a wagonmaker and a blacksmith. On the 5th of July I resumed the journey and proceeded 25 miles up the American fork to the Lower Mines, or Mormon Diggins. The hillsides were thickly strewn with canvas tents and bush arbours. The day was intensely hot, yet about 200 men were at work in the full glare of the sun, washing for gold. The gold in the lower mines is in fine bright scales, of which I send several specimens.

Mr. Marshall was living near the mill, and informed me that the success was ranging there from one to three ounces of gold per man daily. In a bed of small streams, now dry, a great deal of coarse gold has been found. A great many specimens were shown me, some as heavy as four or five ounces, and I send three pieces.

It was Polk's Message to Congress which aroused truly remarkable gold excitement in the eastern and middle states, much as Sam Brannan's display had done earlier in San Francisco...

The accounts of the abundance of gold in that territory are of such an extraordinary character as would scarcely command belief, were they not corroborated by the authentic reports of officers in the public service who have visited the mineral district. His report is laid herewith before Congress. The explorations already made warrant the belief that the supply is very large, and that gold is found in various places in extensive districts of the country.

After that, there was no holding the argonauts back. The astonishing pattern of human movement to California was established. California would never again be sleepy.

The Gold Rush of Forty-Nine turned California into a roaring, boisterous settlement, dominated by the reaping and spending of gold in flamboyant style and prodigious amounts.

As President Polk discovered, it had been all but impossible to get anyone but fur traders to venture west of Missouri until word of gold got around. After that, it was impossible to hold anyone back.

They all took off for the Mines

Some say it was Greed that settled the West. At any rate, it gave those cartoonists and lithographers who stayed home a field day in lampooning the state of greedy hysteria occasioned by the lorelei of gold.

The French view of life at the mines

The German's view of life at the mines

Britains **Punch** magazine pictured a streetsweeper off to the mines. "Oh! I ain't going to stop here looking for teaspoons in cinders. I'm off to Kallifornier, where there's heaps of gold dust to be had for the sweepin'"

They couldn't get there fast enough

"I wish Jemima could see me now, goin' through the Firmament like a streak of greased lightnin' on a telegraph wire. When I get to Californy I'll let others do the diggins while I do the swapping."

Death of a Dream

By all odds, Sutter should have become one of the world's wealthiest men. He owned an immense area of land adjacent to the richest mining camps; he was a successful farmer with fields of grain and vegetables to sell, great herds of cattle and sheep; his fort turned out all kinds of goods sorely needed by miners.

But it all crumbled. He could hold on to none of it.

His workers took off for the gold fields. His wheat rotted in the fields. Looms lay idle. Leather spoiled in tanning vats. His stock strayed through holes in fences broken by trespassers. Hungry miners slaughtered his cows, trampled his crops. It's said that one Sacramento butcher made $60,000 during the winter of 1849-50 dealing in stolen Sutter cattle. Lamented Sutter, "I had no idea people could be so mean."

Sutter himself was psychologically incapable of adjusting to his changed circumstances. He couldn't get past the picture he had created of himself as a swashbuckling land baron managing a feudal estate.

Still playing the gracious host to everyone who came as a guest, he was overwhelmed by the sheer logistics. Even the hospitable act of drinking a welcoming toast of his home-made *aguardiente* with each new visitor was turning him into a semi-alcoholic (he had certainly never been a teetotaler), so that his man-servant frequently put him to bed glazed and incoherent.

All the publicity about his gold fields had put him in another peril. His creditors (and they were many) had previously been satisfied with his explanation that "crops are poor this year." Now they all started demanding immediate payment. The Russians were particularly pressing. The four-year note he gave them for Fort Ross had stretched into seven years, and he was in arrears $19,000. They threatened to seize his Fort.

It was at this point that his far-distant past bobbed up to save him. His first-born son, now 22, appeared unexpectedly at his father's adobe headquarters.

To escape his creditors, Sutter put everything he owned, including the schooner *Sacramento*, in his son's name, and hightailed it out of town to a small farm he had built downriver.

It was no small responsibility he handed a 22-year-old who had been in the country only two months.

In order to pay off the clamoring creditors, John Junior (backed by Sam Brannan and Peter Burnett) had the land fronting the Embarcadero surveyed into lots to establish a townsite. An auction was held on January 8th, and business lots sold briskly at $500 apiece ($250 away from the waterfront). With these funds, the most pressing of his father's creditors debts were paid. It was Brannan who claimed credit for naming the town Sacramento City.

It would seem the elder Sutter would be delighted. As a matter of fact, when he came down from the hills he was furious. It was **his** plan to make Sutterville, his town two miles downriver, the townsite. The power of attorney was rescinded, and the breach between father and son was never really mended.

By the end of 1849 Sutter sold out his installation for $40,000. For the rest of his life he continued to lose money through poor judgment and ill luck.

The end came in Washington, D.C. He was there applying to Congress for a grant he felt he deserved as reimbursement for aid given in years past to California-bound emigrants. The campaign continued for years, until finally, in 1860, it looked as though success was at hand. But it came too late. Sutter died there in Washington, at the age of 77.

John Sutter. Was he noble...or an opportunist? Historian Josiah Royce says, "In character, Sutter was an affable and hospitable visionary, of hazy ideas, with a great liking for popularity and with a mania for undertaking too much."

All that was left of Sutter's Fort when the Forty-Niners moved on.

FOOL'S GOLD

"...a discovery that hasn't been of much benefit to me..."

The excitement of that moment when Marshall saw "something shining" in the tailrace, was almost his last happy moment. None of the gold stuck to his fingers, not even the first piece.

*His sawmill went broke and closed down. He laid claim to mining rights, but was ignored by the greedy prospectors who swarmed over his land. Marshall, a gentle person, couldn't fight the claim jumpers. Trouble broke out between prospectors and Indians, and Marshall bore the brunt of it. As a miner he was unsuccessful; from diggings to diggings he was pursued by frenzied **strangers** who thought he had secret access to where the gold was. He was robbed of his horses.*

Finally he settled down to blacksmithing and drinking. After that it was all downhill.

Adversity magnified his unfortunate personal traits. He saw offenses where none had been intended. All men seemed to turn against him.

In 1872, penniless, he asked the State for a $200-a-month pension "in recognition of his considerable service to the State." He got that but the next year the pension was cut to $100, and then discontinued altogether.

He lived his last seven years alone and in abject poverty, and died alone in his humble cabin. They buried him in Coloma, in soil which had once been his.

The Native Sons of the Golden West erected a monument to him that cost $25,000, and paid a caretaker $75 a month to tend the parkland around it.

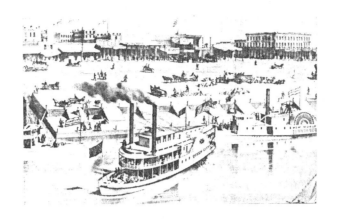

BOOMTOWN ON THE RIVER

By June of that historic year, 1849, the tide of immigration had turned into a flood.

On June 16th the *Placer Times* reported a hundred houses and 25 stores were "already erected and others going up rapidly." Two weeks later (to show how rapid that development was) it announced, "Sacramento now has 2,000 inhabitants and about 200 houses. A large and magnificent hotel is being built by Sam Brannan."

And the lots that the junior John Sutter had sold with such satisfaction for $500 in January, now commanded $5,000.

The first houses that sprang up beyond J Street came with the emigrants from "the States", shipped around the Horn. Said pioneer J.M. Betts, "In July of 1849 there was about 100 houses and tents in town. It seemed like every man landed with a house and put it up the same day. Our brig had no less than 13 on board, finished even to the glazing."

It was a great time to be a merchant.

Prices were inflated shamelessly by every shopkeeper. Nevertheless, trade with the miners increased with such incredible rapidity that it promised a certain fortune to anyone with something to sell. Sales amounted to thousands daily; clerks made salaries from $300 to $500 a month, and few could be retained long at that.

Saloons flourished, of course.

According to contemporary historian, John Morse, "The first saloon keeper in town was an enterprising individual who took a sail from a ship tied at the Embarcadero, wrapped it around three times, put a plank across two barrels and "opened" an hour after his arrival. When early summer's heat had reached the saltstained canvas walls, miners dubbed his saloon the "Stinking Tent."

Sacramento Union, Jan. 29, 1864...
Several Sutter Creekers were in town yesterday, who seemed determined to enjoy themselves. Having provided themselves with horses they rode around town and called occasionally at their headquarters, the Pavillion Saloon. Being in an unfit condition to dismount, they made it a point to ride their horses into the saloon by one door, take their liquor, and then ride out the other. No particular damage was done by the proceeding.

"A fearful picture of the state of society," the London Daily News said of the El Dorado Gambling Hall at 2nd and J

Gambling also flourished, here as elsewhere that miners gathered. Away from the family fireside, and with few other public gathering places, it became an all-absorbing pursuit.

Gamblers became important public figures, and many became possessed of great wealth and influence. So much so, that for a short time they controlled the destiny of the new city. At the election for Sheriff in 1849, a gambler was elected in preference to a solid citizen.

Prospectors, still dusty from the diggins, brought their heavy sacks of dust and nuggets to the Gem, the Humboldt, the Empire and laid them on the monte tables, where there were tiny scales to weigh the bets.

Monte was the favorite game of the times, but there were others. "Lucky Bill" Thorington stationed himself at Lee's Exchange, largest of Sacramento's gambling houses, and extracted $24,000 in sixty days from willing victims with his shell game.

"Here, gentlemen, is a nice, quiet game," was his come-on. "It's recommended by the clergy for its honesty and wholesome moral tendencies. I win only from blind men; all that have two good eyes can win a fortune."

Gambling wasn't confined to standard games like monte, faro, and fantan. An entrepreneur in Sacramento who purchased a herd of camels he thought might be useful as pack animals in Nevada, decided to pick up a little extra money by staging a Dromedary Race.

Sacramentans were enchanted. The beasts were taken to a fenced oval race track, and after heavy betting by spectators, were prodded into running. There were no jockeys. Each camel carried a placard bearing a number.

The race started out well enough, the camels humping right along. But at the first turn every camel elected to sink to its knees. More prodding. More cussing. The camels reluctantly resumed the silly race.

At the second turn they all sank to their knees once again. And this time no amount of cussing or bullwhipping would make them change their minds.

Arguments over settlement of the bets lasted for years.

But gambling halls were not profitable for the naive, and many a migrant found that the saloons offered poor whiskey and poorer entertainment. To add a touch of class to recreation, the Eagle Theater was built on Front Street, first of its kind in California.

Entrance to the theater was through the Round Tent Saloon next door, where patrons purchased their tickets, generally pouring out a quantity of gold valued by the ticket seller at $12 an ounce. The balcony could also be reached (for those who disdained the gambling saloons) by the way of a ladder outside the theater, primly shielded by a canvas tacked underneath for the benefit of the ladies.

Finding a troupe of actors 2,000 miles from cultured civilization was no small assignment. The first member recruited was John Bowman Atwater, a roving actor who arrived in the city broke and barefoot. Then a local merchant, Herman Cardwell, who had once acted with Atwater in New York, signed up. Most of the remainig troupe came from a disbanded battalion of soldiers passing through town.

The first performance starred Mrs. Henry Ray in "Spectre of the Forest." Fortunately for posterity, a reporter from Horace Greeley's New York *Tribune* chanced to be in town, and wrote a review of this entertaining play.

Dancer Lola Montez, who entertained Sacramento, was once the mistress of King Ludwig of Bavaria

The City Council of 1849 was a hide-and seek body — like everything else in California at that time, very changeable. The minutes for October indicate that White was elected to replace Sloat, who had left town. Glashins replaced Harper, who had resigned. Snyder replaced McLelland. There were three more changes in November. In December, hoping to encourage some permanency, the Council passed an ordinance paying themselves $100 a month salary, which proved very unpopular with the constituency.

By the end of 1849, Sacramento was no longer an outpost.

The overture commences; the orchestra is composed of five members, under the direction of an Italian, and performs with tolerable correctness. The piece for the night is "The Spectre of the Forest" in which the celebrated actress, Mrs. Ray of the Royal Theater, New Zealand, will appear. The bell rings. The curtain rolls up, and we look upon a forest scene. Mrs. Ray rushes in and throws herself into an attitude in the middle of the stage. Why she does it no one can tell. This movement, which she repeats several times in the course of the first three acts, has no connection with the tragedy; it is evidently introduced for thr purpose of showing the audience that there is actually a female performer. The miners, to whom the sight of a woman is not a frequent occurrence, are delighted with the passages and applaud vehemently.

1849 portrays a city with well defined streets, with many structures lining the waterfront, including hotels, stores, saloons and a theater. The river bank and embarcadero are bustling with people, animals, ships, and goods being transported to the world.

Sacramento had moved from wilderness to city in a brief ten years.

SACRAMENTO SUBMERGED

"I had always been opposed to the plan of establishing the metropolis of the valley at the Embarcadero. The location was favorable enough, to be sure, but the land was so low that a rise of the river above normal would cause a flood in the town. For this very reason, I started the town of Sutterville, high above the level of the river."

...Capt. John Sutter

A rising river is an awesome thing. There is so little anyone can do about it.

December of 1849 had been a soggy month for Sacramento. Every day, it seemed, brought more rain; frequent downpours pelted the city. As an old-timer put it, "it just kept comin' and a-comin'."

By January the saturated ground could soak up no more. Both the American and Sacramento rivers had reached the brim of their banks. And when, on the evening of Janaury 8th, another batch of water was dispatched from the heavens above, the city was inundated. Sacramento became a lake several feet deep.

Oddly, no one was prepared for disaster.

"People came floating out of their habitations on beds and boxes and in every conceivable condition. Some were mounted on top of their houses, and remained in such rather precarious positions for a long time. Merchandise of every description came floating on the tide.

> There were many deaths in the 1850 flood, so that a Dutchman with a boat had to be hired to take them away to be buried.
>
> The Dutchman, suspicious of everyone, always carried his money (in the form of gold dust) with him, strapped to his waist. He had about $2,000 worth when, unfortunately, he made a mistake and placed the coffin across a very small boat. In deep water the boat started careening and finally overturned. He shouted to his helper to hold on, he would swim ashore and get a larger boat. The gold dust was heavy; it drew him under. With a tremendous struggle, he came up again and again, but finally sank and was drowned.
>
> His helper floated ashore on the coffin, which happened to be made very tight.

There were not a half dozen stores whose doors were above the water line, while in some it reached the ceiling. The entrance to City Hotel was from boats through the second story window.

Most sad was the plight of abandoned hospital patients, wrapped in blankets and floating around on their beds.

The only dry spots in town were Sutter's Fort, the R Street levee, City Plaza on J Street (crowded with domestic animals), and an abrupt hill rising east of 20th street called Poverty Ridge.

Mercifully the deluge stopped, and a week later everyone was piling out of the debris, getting back to normal, selling goods to miners.

There was an irrepressible spirit of rosy optimism in the days of Forty-Nine. Once danger had passed, no one seemed to give it another thought. It never occurred to anyone it could happen again. No one except Hardin Bigelow, that is.

When heavy rains started hitting again in March, Bigelow was down at the waterfront building a levee, and plaguing everyone else to pitch in and help, though they thought he was crazy. As a result of his hard-headed persistence, Bigelow saved the city. And the city rewarded Bigelow by making him its first mayor.

"Notwithstanding universal destruction, an irresistible disposition to laugh was manifested, and each satisfied himself that he was at least as well off as his neighbor. People were not content with being wet outside, but bent on wetting the inside too."

After the flood water receded, the occupants of tents and shanties on the high ground refused to evacuate. In those times, no one paid the slightest respect to land title if it conflicted in any way with his own interest.

A squatter named Robinson had put together some sort of shack on a stretch of levee on I Street, and it was interfering with unloading of goods. He was standing in the doorway, evidently impressed with the principle that every man's home is his castle, when Sam Brannan rode up in frenzied excitement, with a group of men intent on removing squatters from the Sacramento scene. As Brannan grabbed hold of a portion of the building and started yanking at it, the owner displayed a shotgun, saying, "Hold on sir, you touch this house at your peril! It's mine, and I intend to defend it!"

Brannan turned to the nearest of the party and bellowed out, "Warbass, cover that damn scoundrel, and if he raises a gun, shoot the hell out of him!" In a few minutes the shanty had disappered.

By sunset, the "destroying angels" had levelled every shanty in town.

SQUATTERS' WAR

As a matter of fact, the rights of squatters became a matter of great importance in the development of Sacramento.

The gigantic land grants given by the Mexicans to Sutter and others were fine when there weren't more than a dozen men living inland in California.

But with thousands of men pouring into California weekly, it was plainly not going to work for a few men to own the entire state. Even where land had been sold by the grantee speculation was rampant and land prices had skyrocketed.

The new settlers were laying claim to a piece of California on the basis of an old frontier tradition, the right of occupancy... "squatters' rights."

The land speculators, of course, were their opposition.

Dr. Robinson was the leader of the settlers, supported by James McClatchy and Richard Moran who were publishing a small newspaper that supported the right of free soil.

When McClatchy and Moran were jailed, the Free Soilers got their hackles up and marched in a body to the jail, led by a man named Maloney.

Before the march reached the jail, it had turned into a riot. In a wild spree of shooting, Maloney was fatally shot, one of the squatters was shot in the neck, the city assessor was killed by a stray ball, the mayor fell from his horse, and Dr. Robinson was wounded.

Robinson, as leader of the settlers, was jailed and charged with murder. But while he was in the pokey his friends put his name up for election to the State Legislature. While he was waiting trial (which never occurred) he won the election.

 And the squatters won the war.

CAPITOL GAINS

Only two years after Marshall's portentous find, California was admitted as the 31st state of the Union.

For the next five years, the most important business of the State Legislature seemed to be deciding where to set up housekeeping. The state capital was variously designated as Monterey (temporary), San Jose (too Mexican), Vallejo (unsatisfactory accommodations), Benicia (too remote). While bouncing around the state, the legislators would drop in on Sacramento from time to time to borrow the large, substantial courthouse built by the County in 1851.

First courthouse,

It was that courthouse that finally won them over. In 1854 Sacramento became the official (and permanent) capital city.

Before the year was out, the building that had so impressed the legislators burned to the ground. But the county built another, even more impressive than the last.

Second courthouse

Because of the importance of gold, California became a state entity without passing through the preliminary territorial period, simply by inferring that if California weren't admitted to the Union on her own terms, she wasn't going at all. The first constitutional convention meeting in Monterey, didn't even bother to draw up a territorial document; they elected a full slate of state officers, and state government was actually functioning several months before California achieved statehood.

Among the delegates at Monterey was Capt. John Sutter, gathering a few last moments of veneration before his empire disintegrated.

When the session ended, the delegates picked up their $16-a-day expense money and went home — only to discover that the United States wasn't sure that California was such a rich gift after all. Admission to the Union came only after weeks of haggling, and then only on the terms it would be a state without slavery.

> *In 1852 a young man from North Carolina, after spending three years in the Golden State, wrote a vitriolic account of his experiences in a state with "barbarous civilization, licentious morals, crude manners and inclement climate." He called it* **Dreadful California.**
>
> *"The city of Sacramento, so smooth and flat, would be one of the most beautiful in the world but for the lack of sufficient elevation.*
>
> *"At present the legislature meets in this place but that august body is possessed of a remarkably roving disposition, having held its sessions at four different places within the last four years at an extra expense to the State of nearly two hundred thousand dollars.*
>
> *"There is no capitol or state house, nor is it likely that California will ever be able to build one while its finances are so recklessly managed. No one here can be successful unless he assimilates himself to the people. He must carouse with villains, attend Sunday horse races, and adapt himself to depravity.*
>
> *Of course there are a few exceptions. Some men, thank heaven, have an innate abhorrence of every thing that savors of meaness or vulgarity."*

It seemed inappropriate that such a rich state shouldn't have a capitol building. So in 1856 the legislature passed a bill authorizing $300,000 to build a capitol on the Plaza square which had been deeded to the city by John Sutter, Jr. when he was managing his father's affairs.

Alas, times were not prosperous, the state was in debt, and decided to abandon the project, and stay on as a renter at the County Courthouse.

Meanwhile, the County became a somewhat reluctant landlord; it now needed the space for its own use. Rather than serve an eviction notice, it deeded to the State the four-block plot from L to N, between 10th and 11th. $500,000 was appropriated, and the work commenced — just in time for the 1862 flood.

It was another twelve years before the building was fully completed. The final tab: over two million dollars.

But an eager populace couldn't wait for the finishing touches to celebrate. In December 1869 the legislative chambers were turned into ballrooms, illuminated by hundreds of gas burners, for the social event of the decade — the Capitol Ball.

"The leaders of fashion from almost every portion of the State were present," reported *Alta California*, San Francisco's leading newspaper. "They were attired in a manner to bewilder the average man. The toilet and jewels worn by one lady are said to represent upwards of $30,000."

At midnight, supper tables in the long corridor on the first floor were unveiled, with "luxuries in quantity profuse," said the *Union*. "The viands having been done justice to, the party returned to the dancing halls and tripped the light fantastic until early morning."

The Capitol's portico columns weren't installed until three years later, and after that the dome was completed. The architect insisted the only proper ornament for the dome was a statue, and fought a valiant but losing battle against "the little round top with the gilt ball" which he described as "simply ridiculous and abominable, a slur on our tastes forever."

In 1906 the Capitol was remodeled, brought up to date with modern plumbing, wiring, and two elevators. Lost in the renovation were the 45 fireplaces that once heated the building, and the iron hitching rings at the carriage entrance.

In 1878 a legislative committee undertook a study of night life with the idea of enacting legislation against sin. Nothing, apparently, came of the research.

At that, talk of moving the capital elsewhere hadn't ended. In 1908 Berkeley decided it would like a turn. The movement was launched be the Berkeley Chamber of Commerce through their senator.

The reasons given for making the change concerned centers of population, difficulty in transportation, and the "picturesque location" provided at Berkeley.

However, problems developed when several other communities, such as Modesto, San Mateo and Santa Cruz wanted it to be located in their town.

The battle became so bitter that several sought to inject a note of humor. A correspondent from Fiddletown wrote: "Let the legislators find out it's a 'dry town' and it's all up with Berkeley. You might as well try to induce a duck to live on the Sahara as get a legislator to move the capital to a town where whiskey can't be bought."

One Senator introduced a bill authorizing the expenditure of $200,000 to build an automobile large enough to move the capitol from place to place "at the whim of disgruntled politicians and real estate boomers." The state legislature sidestepped the issue by voting to submit the proposition to the people in the November election. Voters defeated the proposition two to one.

Once again, in 1941, an attempt was made to transfer the capital. This time Monterey wanted it. But the measure went down in quick defeat.

The Hook & Ladder crew... brave men, valiant firefighters, first on the scene with the water

THE LOOK OF THE TIMES

Wells Fargo...waiting for the gold to come in

This scene in front of Adams & Co. shows the miserable state of street repair

Marshall Rose (left) and his son (rear) operated a machine shop at 9th and K

Hank Fisher came from Dutch Flat in 1862 and built a candy store on J Street

life at china slough

Not every emigrant to the wonderful city of Sacramento found happiness. On a February morning in 1864 a Chinaman was found hanging from an oak near 8th, his neck shielded from the burn of the rope with a handkerchief. In his pocket was a note written Chinese: "I came from the mountains to this city, could not find any friend, any house or place to go to, and I hang myself between the sky and the ground and make myself dead." He was 28 years old.

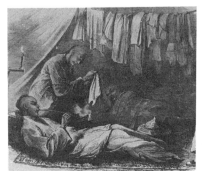

Swamped (again)

In 1862 it happened again. Sacramento was inundated. Worse, this time, than ever before.

Year after year, talk had gone on and on ... and on ... about building up the levees. But since no one could agree on just how high was high, things remained at checkmate. There were even some of the opinion it would be best to simply abandon the whole town where it stood and start over again on higher ground.

Capt. Sutter, wherever he was, must have been enjoying an exquisite I-told-you-so.

Eventually the high-water problem was resolved ... not by one solution, but several. Some were quite incredible.

The levees were raised, of course. Then dredged-out dirt from the American River was hauled into town, and every street in town was raised—more than ten feet in some instances. Sidewalks had to be raised.

And then the buildings (by now sitting in sort of "cellar" below street level) were jacked up, inch by inch, until they appeared to be standing on stilts.

It was a project of staggering proportions. And while work was in progress, residents found it a bewildering and unnerving experience to walk around town, ascending and descending to various levels -- sometimes unexpectedly.

By 1873 the entire downtown city had been raised twelve feet.

Although rowboats were at a premium during the flood of 1863 (and any man who owned one got rich), legislators insisted on being rowed to the Capitol at State expense. Said one Senator, "I think I'm doing my duty, and my whole duty, when I eat only one meal a day, cold at that, in a garret room, and shin down an awning post to get into a boat to go to work." The **Union** *was disgusted, and editorialized, "Men were ready to sacrifice the State because they couldn't keep their boats polished, and because the little buildings in the back yards were overwhelmed in the waters."*

pioneer children

The answer to education of the young in the city's early years was an assortment of private schools, starting in '49 with a flimsy schoolhouse with framing of old lumber, and canvas walls made from an old sail. The Rev. C.T.H. Palmer made a valiant effort as its schoolmaster, but after a month he quit. Later the Reverend Benton took on its four pupils. But by the first of December, weather was too much for the canvas, dirt-floor schoolhouse and he had to close down.

Private schools continued to flourish in astounding numbers for such a small settlement. By 1856 there was a young lady's seminar (60 pupils), a Catholic school, a German school, French school, two "colored" schools, a Hebrew school, and two private high schools.

Sixth grade class of '88.

The high school grads of '73 display a problem common in early days of cameras. Unskilled in the art of posing, they find difficulty in finding suitable position for the hands.

The Traveling Type-Case

The first two newspapers in California were printed in San Francisco—the *Californian*, printed on an old hand-press which had been discarded by the Mexican provincial government...and the *California Star*, Sam Brannan's paper. They were bitter rivals, as might be gathered by an announcement made in Mormon elder Brannan's paper...

"We have received two late numbers of the *Californian*, a dim, dirty little paper... published and edited by a lying sycophant and an overgrown lickspittle."

Both papers missed the journalistic blockbuster of the age; neither one made capital of Marshall's gold discovery. When they did get around to printing the story, the Rush was attacked as "all sham, a superb take-in."

Two days after Brannan made his historic announcement in the streets of San Francisco, both papers suspended publication; their printers had dropped their type-sticks and grabbed up gold pans.

Meanwhile, the *Californian's* doddering old press was packed upriver to New Helvetia, there to produce the *Placer Times* in a small building near Sutter's Fort, under the direction of Editor Edward Kemble and James McClatchy.

At the end of 1860 California had about a hundred newspapers. Sixty competed for readership, at one time or another, in Sacramento. But the journalistic graveyard was a busy place; the only two to survive the battlefield were the *Union* and the *Bee*.

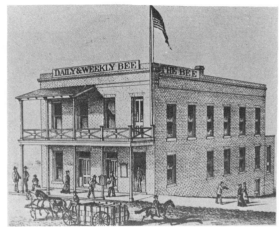

When the dynamic McClatchy left the *Placer Times* and edited the *Bee*, the paper was anything but a drone. McClatchy, once the champion of free soil during the Squatters Riots, now became the champion of small farmers against the powerful cattle and mining interests.

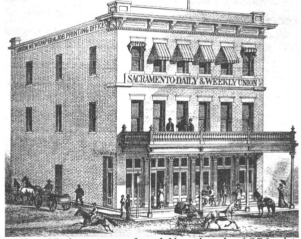

The *Union* started publication in 1851. At a time when there were no schools of journalism, and most frontier newsmen had little formal training, the *Union* had a remarkably well-educated editor, Dr. J. F. Morse, whose 1853 history of Sacramento became a classic.

Like most early newspapers, the *Union's* front page was half editorial, half advertising, and Mellinger's Miracle Medicine competed with Civil War news for the attention of readers.

BROAD, PLACID HIGHWAY

"There is no sound in the world so filled with mystery and longing and unease as the sound at night of a river boat blowing for the landing — one long, two shorts, one long, two shorts...the sound of the river boat hangs inside your heart like a star.'

Capt Sutter didn't know, when he floundered his way through the maze of sloughs and estuaries leading to his dreamed-of empire, that within ten years the tortuous route would become a superhighway.

In the beginning, it was Sutter's schooner *Sacramento* that made frequent trips to San Francisco and Bodega Bay. Sometimes there wasn't a pound of freight to send down, but it was the only way to get mail.

But with the invention of Mr. Fulton's fabulous steamboat a new fleet took over the river. Forerunner of the steamers was the Russian-made *Sitka*. It made one run...San Francisco to Sacramento and back. It took a week getting in. The return trip may have been slower; an oxcart leaving at the same time got to Benicia four days ahead of the steamer.

It didn't matter much. No one was in any great hurry to get to Sacramento, or to leave.

Gold changed that. Suddenly there weren't enough boats in the West to get the frantic prospectors to the mines.

> *An unusual item of freight on the early steamer runs was cats — common cats. Rats were such a plague at the diggings that their feline enemies sold for twenty-five dollars.*

When the steamer *McKim* arrived in October 1849 it was greeted with a salute of cannons and the hurrahs of the inhabitants. She had 60 berths for passengers, who paid $5 for a night's sleep, plus $30 for cabin pasage. Dinner cost $1.50

Four months later, the side-wheeler *Senator* arrived on the scene, and for the next two decades made an every-other-day trip, leaving San Francisco at 2 p.m. on a ten-hour run, heading back the next morning at nine. On early trips, she was jammed with prospectors eager to pay $45 to $65 for the 125-mile voyage, and loaded with freight. She could gross perhaps $50,000 for a one-way trip. Although competition quickly put an end to such lush profits, before this happened the *Senator* probably earned more money than any steamboat in history.

One of the earliest steamships on the river, the Rambler

It is almost impossible, now, to imagine the gigantic proportions of traffic on the river. Sacramento was the center of banking and express between the diggins and San Francisco. On one 1850 day, there were 46 ships on the south bank, 18 on the north. The fame of the Sacramento River was world-wide. Eastern shipbuilders were turning out steamers for this lucrative market at a frenzied pace (at one time 200 were on their way west), until the waters of California were filled. The bonanza ended for them, however, when Yolo went into shipbuilding.

In time the steamboats became downright luxurious. The swift and graceful *Antelope*, queen of the river packets, was known as "The Gold Boat" because of the vast sums in treasure it transported on its downriver run. In April 1860 the first Pony Express rider threw his saddlebags aboard the *Antelope*, and she streaked downstream to complete the coast-to-coast mail service.

But the most fabulous of them all was the *Chrysopolis* (Greek for Golden City), carrier of the elite, aristocrat of the river trade. An English writer described the luxury for the folks back home: "The upper saloon resembles a large hall in an English country home, furnished in the style and with the taste of a splendid drawing room."

With so many boats on the waters, it was inevitable that stiff competition had its effect on the fares. Within a year the rate had tumbled from thirty dollars to ten, to five, to one, sometimes to no charge at all. One stubborn case was reported where the line actually paid passengers to take passage. The solution was an association, the California Steam Navigation Company, which stabilized fares at ten dollars.

When Sacramento became the western terminus of the transcontinental railway, passengers bound for San Francisco left the train and crossed the levee to waiting steamers. The accounts of early-day travelers rarely fail to express suprise at finding ships of such size and luxury at what to them was still a remote frontier town.

But eventually the California Steam Navigation Company, bowing to the demands of a rapidly advancing civilization, sold out to Central Pacific. The railroad continued to operate the popular runs for a number of years, carrying passengers and freight. But in the end, the automobile and the truck defeated river travel. And a long and bitter Longshoremen's strike in San Francisco gave it the final blow.

The luxurious "floating palaces" no longer had a place. The *Chrysopolis* was rebuilt as a double-ender by C.P., renamed the *Oakland*, and set to shuttling back and forth between Oakland and San Francisco as a ferry.

An era in California history had drawn to a close.

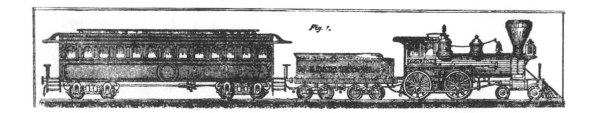

Fig. 1.

SHORTLINE TO GREATNESS

The first railroad west of the Rockies was a short line that ran from Sacramento to Folsom —the Sacramento Valley Railroad.

It wasn't intended to be quite that short. Originally it was planned to run to Marysville. But money was tight that year. And when the bills mounted over the million-dollar mark, everyone agreed that the sight of a train chugging into the Folsom station was indeed a very inspiring thing.

But that 22-mile line opened the door to events of epic proportions. It sparked into prominence its builder, Theodore Judah, a brilliant young engineer with an obsession to build a transcontinental railroad. His plan for the Central Pacific Railway became one of the engineering marvels of the time, crossing the Sierras over grades then thought impossible.

By the time Judah had completed the Sacramento Valley line, he was entranced by his ambition. He researched the engineering technicalities intensively. With his own funds he made survey trips to investigate the most propitious path across the mountains. In off-hours, he made survey trips to San Francisco and Sacramento businessmen to solicit enthusiasm and funds for his project.

San Francisco refused him. It seems likely they saw Sacramento as the terminus city, and weren't anxious to help catapult a rival into fame and fortune.

In Sacramento he had better luck. Among those who came to hear him lecture was a local hardware dealer named Collis Huntington. The money-making possibilities of such a project excited him. And he was able to convince three others—his partner, Mark Hopkins; a grocer named Leland Stanford, and Charles Crocker—to join him in the venture and raise the necessary capital.

The Huntington & Hopkins hardware store on K Street cornered the market in shovels and blasting powder, for which the forty-niners paid dearly

This foursome came, in time, to be known as the Big Four. Their names forever after were linked to the grandest railroad monopoly of all time.

The railroad's planner and architect, the precocious Theodore Judah, who originated the idea and found the route, who arranged the backing, and lobbied Congress with dogged persistence for a contract, is almost forgotten.

> "Here comes Crazy Judah!"
> Even his best friends considered him a fanatic. He was studious, industrious, resourceful, opinionated, humorless, and extraordinarily competent. He was an eccentric whose condition was complicated by a touch of genius.
> Irrevocably, every discussion he started swung around to a subject he found completely fascinating, the ultimate railroad that would span the continent. He then became a man bewitched and hypnotized, dazzled by the magnitude of the conception.

In October of 1863, the year that construction of the Central Pacific started at Sacramento, Judah set sail for New York, contracted Panama fever at the Isthmus, and died a few days later. He was 38 years old.

Penny-pinching Collis Huntington, who had just gone to the expense of building a transcontinental railroad, declared this shack was good enough for Sacramento's depot.   He had it nailed together in a single afternoon, at a cost of $150

> Sacramento **Union** business news, March 16, 1869: By the noon train of the Central Pacific today a large number of gentlemen reached the city, who had been 28 to 32 days en route from New York. Among them were Col. James, formerly controller of San Francisco, William Grim and Frank Rhoads of this place. The trip has been tedious and severe, and they unite in condemning the present condition of the Central Pacific. They say the snow drifts and fills the cuts so compact and solid as to resemble ice and it returns as rapidly as removed.

Frank Leslie, publisher of the popular Leslie's Illustrated Newspaper, set out on a grand tour of the American West in 1877. He took along a gorgeous wife, a half-dozen artists, a Skye terrier, and an ample supply of champagne. With his private car riding behind the overland train, he peeked into *Life* in the wild, wild West, and reported everything he saw to his magazine's readers. He found Virginia City "desolate, homeless, wicked and Godforsaken." In Cheyenne, "promiscuous shooting is becoming quite rare..." In San Francisco, "we certainly saw very elegant toilets."

When the train stopped for a half-hour in Sacramento, Leslie got out and explored.

"Shall we ever forget that half-hour in Sacramento? Under that blue midsummer sky, in that clear atmosphere and soft, bracing, flower-scented air, it seems to us the very most delectable spot that man might ever call home. It looks so quaint and foreign, with its low, wide buildings and wooden arcades, its great, broad, sunny streets, planked sidewalks. Oh, there never were such homes and such gardens as we see in Sacramento! Every street down which we whirl is shadier and prettier and more picturesque than the last; every cottage just a little more enticing to eyes that have looked at the bare Plains and the savage mountain passes for so many days.

"After a fleeting glimpse of a very dirty Chinese quarter and some attractive Chinese bazaars with windows crowded full of curios, we pass some comforable-looking brick hotels with wide verandas and porticoes sheltering the sidewalk; and then we are back at the depot again."

Frank Leslie's artists discover that riding first class was far better than going tourist

That Dashing Pony Rider

Mail from home was a momentous occasion for early Californians. Small wonder. If a letter arrived by ship, it had been three months in transit. Butterfield's Overland Mail, the next progressive step, made it across the plains in only fifty days.

The answer to speedy delivery was the Pony Express.

St. Joe to Sacramento—1980 miles. Eight days.

It required 200 relay stations, 500 horses, 80 riders. Riders were young (under 21), lightweight (no more than 125 pounds), and brave beyond belief. Most of them could outride an Indian, and frequently did. They changed horses every half-hour, vaulting from saddle to saddle with the mail-stuffed *mochila* in hand, not wasting more than two minutes in the exchange. They outwitted road agents and circumvented Indian attacks along the way.

On April 3, 1860 the first Pony Express rider dashed from St. Joseph, Missouri. The next day, rider Harry Roff left Sacramento at the gallop, racing east, and covered the 55 miles to Placerville in three hours. An average ride for each man was supposed to be 35 miles. But later riders often faced stretches of 300 miles, particularly if the next rider was found dead at the station.

It was April 13 when the first rider from St. Joe came pounding in to Sacramento. The town went wild. Streets were decorated with flags, merchants had arranged Pony Express displays in their windows, and banners expressed a variety of stirring sentiments, including, "Pony Express! Russell, Major & Co. take the skates!"

An advance mounted cavalcade was at the edge of town waiting to escort the rider into Sacramento in a blaze of glory—somewhat to the dismay of the courier, who complained that the cavalcade, in their enthusiasm, "dug their spurs into their fresh animals and took the lead, creating a great dust which was not only annoying to me but injurious to my pony."

But that didn't mar the celebration. Jubilant residents went hysterical over the historic event. Firemen boomed a salute with a cannon. An impromptu anvil chorus added to the general celebration. Rider and mail were ceremoniously put aboard the *Antelope* for the last leg of the mail route (though later only the mail made that trip).

The first mail delivery pouch held 80 letters for Sacramento and San Francisco, sent at a rate of $5 a half-ounce.

Arrival of the first Pony Express rider

The Pony Express is such a colorful part of the lore of the West that few people realize how short the span it covered. The most unique and romantic mail service ever organized lasted only 18 months, then was replaced by the telegraph and the railroad.

The tales told by riders like "Pony Bob" Haslam and "Buffalo Bill" Cody have become part of the legend of the western frontier.

Crossing the Nevada desert, Pony Bob recounted, "It was growing dark and my road lay through sagebrush high enough to hide a horse. I kept a bright lookout and watched my pony's ears, which is a signal for danger in Indian country. At Carson I found the station men badly frightened, for they had seen some 50 warriors in warpaint."

Before a Pony Express rider was signed up, he had to promise not to drink, swear, or fight with hostile Indians.

For this, a rider's pay was $100 per month, with bonuses paid for extra speed.

The Pony rider waves to the crew   raising the lines that will replace him

The modern advance that closed the life of the Pony Express was completion of the Overland Telegraph Line, constructed with governmental assistance, which reached Sacramento October 4, 1861. Cost of a telegram from Sacramento to San Francisco: $2 for the first ten words, 75¢ each additional five.

The telegraph was another step in the long struggle to give California speedy communication with the East, in spite of horrendous geographical barriers.

But even the telegraph presented its problems. In 1854 the California State Telegraph Company posted a notice concerning the Auburn-Sacramento line: "The wires of the telegraph near the Fort were broken yesterday by a load of hay passing under them. Persons driving such teams should be very careful while passing beneath ____ s as it is a great public loss when ____ cation between the various cities in ____ is interrupted."

The Linesmen

GETTING IT TOGETHER CIVICALLY

The Great Electric Connection

As early as 1855, Sacramento streets were lit by gas lamps. Not that anyone was terribly impressed. That first year the gas company had 113 customers. Ten years later they had only 600.

When electric street lights were proposed in 1884, that novelty was greeted with apathy. By then everyone was used to gas lamps and opposed giving a franchise to the electric company. Particularly vociferous was the mayor (who happened to be manager of the gas company), who protested that electricity was neither "reliable nor successful." Even the *Bee* and the *Union* weren't sure; they advised citizens not to sign contracts for electrical illumination until they had seen the new gas lights which had eliminated the disagreeable hissing noise generally associated with arc lighting.

But there's no holding back progress. By 1895 a new powerhouse had been built overlooking China Slough, and enthusiasm for electricity was rampant. Someone came up with a great idea, illuminating the Capitol. Then the *Bee* caught the spirit, and topped it with the ultimate: a Great Electric Carnival!

An entire summer was devoted to laying plans for the grand event. On Admission Day, it all came off. Elaborate arches crossed the streets. Special displays made of colored lights were spotted around town. And the Capitol building was dressed in electricity from dome to grounds. Across the west entrance were the names of Morse, Franklin and Edison outlined in incandescent bulbs. "Every tree in Capitol Park bore fruit like the ones in the gardens in the fairy tales," reported the eloquent *Bee* reporter. "Throughout the evening the electric current behaved beautifully. It never wavered in its duties an instant."

At eight o'clock the Grand Marshall stepped out and led the parade down J Street, followed by electric floats drawn by an electric street car getting its current from an overhead trolley. The crowning moment came at the end of the parade. The men of the railroad shops had made twelve floats, each ingenious. One, "Hive of Industry" featured a beehive made of rope with a swarm of electric bees; a tiny girl was dressed as Queen Bee, and at the back of the float was a bear fighting off a swarm of bees.

The San Francisco *Examiner*, dazzled by Sacramento's splendor, reported, "Description gets lost in admiration of the witching delights of this night's brilliant display. The temptation is to pile superlatives as high as the dome of the Capitol."

The Not-so-great Sewer Connection

Progress in the sanitation department, on the other hand, was far from dazzling.

The problem was acknowledged, but simply ignored.

Standing pools of stagnant water around town provided a good dumping ground for everyone's garbage. Astute lot owners usually filled them with dirt as soon as possible so they didn't provide a dumping basin for the property next door. Pity the poor Chinese, who lived along China Slough, which remained unfilled and became an intolerable receptacle for "filthy accumulations," as the *Bee* reported. Action taken was to arrest and prosecute the Chinese residents. Not so easily prosecuted was another offender, the Southern Pacific. As late as 1910 the lake that formed when the river was dredged was still a dumping ground filled with boxes, oil and other debris.

Cesspools in a town the size of Sacramento were, according to the complaint of a health-minded citizen, "the most abominable of all nuisances, frequently without traps to prevent free passage of cesspool air into the house." Homeowners, he said, were anxious for more sanitary conditions, but landlords didn't believe in "new notions about the dangers of filth pots, obstructed drains, poisoned house air, noxious privies and polluted cesspools."

Levees which held water from the river from flowing in, also kept water from the city from flowing out. The drinking water gained the name, "Sacramento Straight", since it came straight from the river without benefit of filtration.

Sacramento didn't obtain sanitary sewers until 1900. And residents continued to drink their water "raw" until a filtration plant was built in 1924.

Making a Phone Connection

The first two Bell telephones in town were installed at Baker & Hamilton, and in the Music Parlor. Not that these businesses needed to call anyone. The phones were used to attract customers.

Nevertheless, once the effectiveness of the telephone was demonstrated, the new contraption caught on quickly.

A novel use for the telephone became very popular: telephonic concerts. Telephone enthusiasts hooked telephones to the telegraph wires, and performed in musical events for the enjoyment of groups gathered at each transmitter. One of the most famous of these concerts took place over a line connecting Sacramento, Marysville, Chico and Red Bluff. The Sacramento station in the telegraph office had 16 receivers, but only one transmitter. An Edison carbon telephone was used, and it was said that the transmitter became so hot "one could scarcely touch it, so powerful was the electric current." Sacramento's contribution to the concert was the Orphan's Choir singing "Sweet and Low."

FINE FARMING LAND

If it was gold mining that spanked Sacramento into life, it was agriculture that sustained it in the years following.

When Capt. Sutter arrived at New Helvetia, trailing his little band of Kanakas, he quickly set to work sowing wheat. For the frontier settler there are no stores, no ready-at-hand groceries. Survival depends on turning the land into food. The hot, dry Sacramento Valley was eminently suited to the growing of wheat, and Sutter's crops prospered, in spite of the serious handicap of being without farm implements.

During the flamboyant years of the Gold Rush, there was never enough wheat to provide bread for the advancing army of prospectors, and flour became preposterously speculative in Sacramento. But by 1856, when things had settled down, California was raising enough for its own needs, and in 1873 it was the largest wheat-producing state in the nation. The Sacramento Valley was called "breadbasket for the world."

Those were the days when Sacramento River barges, or shallow-draft "dew skimming" steamers, took the golden grain down the river to the Bay, which led to the world beyond.

Hay Scows down the Sacramento

Sutter's main source of revenue (aside from the borrowed money he never repaid) was the raising of grain. It took ingenuity to harvest a crop with minimal implements, as John Bidwell discovered when he was a guest at the Fort...

"Harvesting, with the rude implements, was a scene. Imagine three or four hundred wild Indians in a grain field, armed, some with sickles, some with butcher knives, some with pieces of hoop iron roughly fashioned into shapes like sickles, but many having only their hands with which to gather by small handfuls the dry willow sticks, which were split to afford a sharper edge with which to sever the straw.

"But the wildest part was the threshing. The harvest of weeks, sometimes of a month, was piled up in the straw in the form of a huge mound in the middle of a high, strong, round corral; then three or four hundred wild horses were turned in to thresh it, the Indians whooping to make them run faster. Suddenly they would dash in before the band at full speed, when the motion became reversed, with the effect of plowing up the trampled straw to the very bottom. In an hour the grain would be throughly threshed and the dry straw broken almost into chaff. In this manner I have seen two thousand bushels of wheat threshed in a single hour.

"Next came the winnowing, which would often take another month. It could only be done when the wind was blowing, by throwing high into the air shovelfuls of grain, straw, and chaff, the lighter materials being wafted to one side, while the grain, comparatively clean, would descend and form a heap by itself. In this manner all the grain in California was cleaned."

But in the 1880's Australia and Canada began to pour their crops onto the world's market, and the price of wheat dropped drastically. That's when Sacramento farmers decided to look into the profits of raising fruits and vegetables. For the small farmer it proved to be a wise move, for it was difficult for a man owning less than a thousand acres to compete with the wheat barons. Whereas raising grain required a $20,000 investment in land, machinery and teams, $5,000 would produce an orchard or vineyard to yield at least a moderate living.

Thus began the sprawling orchards of plums, pears, and peaches that proliferated Sacramento's outlying reaches—lands that would later become towns with names like Carmichael (once the Deterding ranch), and Fair Oaks, and Citrus Heights.

> *A 1900 advertisement in the Sacramento* **Bee** *touted Fair Oaks as "the paradise of the fruit grower, health seeker, and tourist. Property now selling at $100 to $200 an acre."*

> *Earlier pioneers had also seen the possibilities of fruit trees in Sacramento. George Schwartz, who obtained a Mexican grant in 1844, planted several acres of watermelons in 1849 and made $30,000 in one year. A. S. Greenlaw, who had 35 acres near 14th and D, harvested cherries from a boat during the 1863 floods.*

The new small crop industry brought Sacramento another problem—racial discrimination, and in an unexpected quarter, the Japanese.

The first Japanese agricultural workers came to help harvest fruit in Vacaville, and were such good workers that they became in great demand in the Sacramento Valley. Their numbers increased slowly for the next few years; but when the U.S. annexed Hawaii in 1898, ten thousand young Japanese men arrived.

The arrangement the newcomers had with the farmer is that they would work for him, but also lease part of his land for their own farming. Before long, the Japanese had acquired some 83,000 acres. Farmers were beginning to wonder if the idea had been a good one; now the hired help was in competition, and in some cases doing better than the farmer. Japanese were producing 80% of the canning tomatoes, 61% of asparagus, and 78% of the spinach crop in the Sacramento region.

It was hardly fair, but in 1913 the Alien Land Law was passed, prohibiting anyone who had been born in Japan from owning California land.

> *The first successful commercial fruit cannery in Sacramento was the Capitol Packing Company at Front and K Streets. As early as 1882 they were advertising themselves as "packers of hermetically sealed goods." In the first year of business, 400 workers canned 40,000 cases of fruit, honey, asparagus and salmon — "without a single can spoiling."*

In the 1920's a new financial institution came on the scene that proved to be a boon to the farmer, the Bank of Italy (later Bank of America). Valley farmers had always been financially handicapped because agriculture requires short term loans, such as those which enable a farmer to expand his cultivated acreage, or tide him over a bad year. Those loans hadn't been available from local banks at reasonable interest because local banks didn't have access to savings in city banks. Better financial support contributed substantially to the growth of agriculture in the Valley, and thus to the prosperity of the city.

GOING STRONG

As the century turned, Sacramento was becoming downright metropolitan.

The City Treasurer found enough money in the budget to sign a contract for a new City Hall — solid granite, the interior lined with marble, with floor-to-ceiling bronze entrance doors that were so heavy it took two strong men to open for business each morning. The price tag: $173,900.

The State Treasurer, too, opened up his heart and his bank account, to buy the Governors of the State a permanent residence. It cost him $32,500 (unfurnished) to buy the old Gallatin home. George Pardee was the first Governor to live in the house, followed by a succession of men who got there on a platform of cutting budget and improving services. There was Hiram Johnson, a feisty little man who didn't want the job but gave it all he had...and Friend Richardson, a Quaker who managed to accumulate $14 million in the Treasury by "constant resistance to spendthriftiness." Later came "Sunny Jim" Rolph, elected as a "wet" in Prohibition days. In all, thirteen governors made the elegant Victorian at 16th and H Streets their home, before Governor Reagan balked at its inconvenience.

The River continued to be a major highway. In 1908, 150,000 passengers made the 12-hour trip from Sacramento to San Francisco on boats owned by the Southern Pacific. River freight dropped, early in the 1900's, when farmers quit raising wheat, but it picked up again in 1910, stronger than ever, until warehouses and wharves had to be added all along the river. By 1925 Sacramento had become the second most important river port in the United States.

Bicycling was still going strong (though it died out when the automobile became popular). The Capitol City Wheelmen joined the "Good Roads Movement," and their enthusiasm contributed significantly to the fact Sacramento County had some of the best roads in the state.

The Capitol City Wheelmen did more than bicycle; their social functions were such gala affairs that some people joined the club who didn't even own a bicylcle.

A couple of San Francisco lawyers named Haggin and Tevis acquired Rancho Del Paso, a 44,000-acre Spanish land grant given to Eliah Grimes in 1844, for $5,000 on a foreclosure sale. They turned it into a racehorse farm (the largest in the world), devoted to producing champions from the best breeding stock. But in 1905 Haggin gave up the business, declaring it was unprofitable, and besides, as he said, it was "a dangerous occupation, for it fosters the worst habit of people, the habit of gambling, which begins in the majority of cases on racetrack tips." Five years later he sold his "unprofitable" $5,000 ranch for $1.5 million. (It is now home for over 100,000 people in North Sacramento, Del Paso Manor, Arden Park, Town & Country, and Del Paso Heights.)

The opening of the elegant new Bank of America at 6th and K in June of 1923 brought crowds of properly impressed citizens

The business community was expanding. The city's first life insurance company was formed — California Western Life —occupying a suite of ten offices on which the rent was $216 a month. Three stenographers and a bookkeeper each commanded a monthly salary of $75; the telephone girl and the office boy had to get by on $40. The first mortgage loan made by the company was for $1,200.

Prices were low. You could get a set of false teeth for 8 dollars.

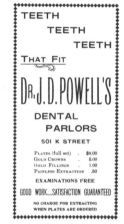
The automobile had made its appearance, terrifying horses and mystifying pedestrians. In the beginning the new mechanical contraption was little more than a toy for the rich; but after Henry Ford created the Model T in 1908, autos and motorcycles became a common sight on Sacramento streets. Cost of road maintenance went up; in 1904 the amount expended was $84,904.

Sometimes a horse was more maneuverable.

Population was up to 50,000. And the Chamber of Commerce bragged that Sacramento had "an equable climate, summer nights cool; no sunstroke, snow nor blizzard."

The first transcontinental airmail plane arrived at Mather in 1925, heralding the start of regular airmail service. When the plane took off for San Francisco, a moving picture company, on location in Sacramento for the filming of "Pony Express", had one of its actors gallop a horse down the runway after the plane to emphasize the contrast in mail service.

The Depression that struck the nation with a 20,000-volt jolt in 1929 had its effect on Sacramento, too. Business was down, unemployment up. But the economy was agricultural, and by and large the ill effect may have been less severe than it was in manufacturing communities.

Businessmen re-grouped, trying to find some tunnel out of the hole that would lead to Prosperity. Some of the schemes were nothing short of spectacular. One avenue of alleviating hardship was to bring back 2.75% beer — which, it was claimed, would "aid agriculturists and revive employment." Another great idea (and one which worked) was to ask every resident in the city to contract for some household repair within ninety days. Within three weeks the total pledged amounted to almost $2 million in services.

A bigger boost to the economy came in the form of a Public Works project to build a new Post Office.

It was a building to be proud of, a classic of Art Noveau, in the style of the Empire State Building. Its marble walls were profusely trimmed in aluminum embossed with a Federal eagle motif. The elevator doors were panels of patterned aluminum. And the ceiling was a geometric wonder of molded plaster of paris painted in silver and gold.

Governor "Sunny Jim" Rolph incensed the populace in 1933 by signing a legislative bill for sales tax (including a tax on food), but vetoing a bill for income tax. His stand on taxation appeared clear: soak the poor, but give the rich a break.

If the Depression was a strain on survival at times, Sacramentans, like the rest of the nation, found some solace in the theaters, where movies cost a dime or a quarter. They gave away dishes; they conducted talent shows. And for a brief time they offered wedding presents to any couple who would come up on the stage and get married.

Sacramento survived the Depression, and it survived a State of War.

The announcement of the Japanese attack on Pearl Harbor had a particularly poignant effect on Sacramento because of the large Japanese population that had been attracted by agriculture. One by one, and in truckloads, the Japanese were removed from their foothold on J Street and herded off to internment camp. Their businesses were closed, their houses evacuated. When they returned after the War had ended, the government would give them 15¢ on the dollar for what they had left behind.

Mather grew, McClellan grew.

And to entertain the servicemen, the Sacramento Civic Theater was born. The first short play (with a cast of four) was taken to Mather, and received such an enthusiastic response that a bigger production was trouped to Mather and McClellan, then on to Camp Kohler and anywhere servicemen could be found.

When the War was over, Sacramento had grown. It would grow more, for servicemen who had left their farms in Iowa, their jobs in New Jersey, had found out about the great state of California, and the pleasant life of Sacramento. For many, it was to become a home for the future.

In fact, in time Sacramento would boast the third largest concentration of military retirees in the nation.

A CITY PROUD

As it often happens, the growth of Sacramento took the town center away from the River, away from the old streets where dynamic Sam Brannan had sold miners' pans and battled floods and where the Pony Express had charged in on streets laid out by John Sutter, Jr.

And as the new city moved eastward, the old city turned derelict, abandoned by commerce, no longer comfortable for decent citizens to call home. Old buildings that had been brought around the Horn in the 1850's, to be erected in the new golden land, deteriorated and became, the hangout of thieves, prostitutes, drunks and common rats. One 12-block area, in particular, had 167 bars and wine shops. Fires and crimes were commonplace.

In 1951 the City Council took action.

The Redevelopment Agency that was established in that year is one of the most remarkable in the country — because it works. In many cities there's much rhetoric, little action. In Sacramento there's very little talk, but a lot gets done.

By 1956 the first of the derelict properties had been acquired. The following year demolition began. All of M Street leading from the river, formerly an ugly avenue of deterioration, was levelled. Miraculously, the entrance to Sacramento from the West was transformed from an eyesore into a remarkably beautiful curtain-raiser to the city beyond, a landscaped avenue lined with handsome office buildings.

The Chinese sector fronting on I Street was turned from blight to beauty by creating a Chinese Cultural Center, a mall with modern apartment buildings and restaurants, hotels.

Downtown shopping plazas have replaced broken-down saloons. Modern office buildings now rise on streets that were once Skid Row.

Perhaps the most remarkable of projects of the Redevelopment Agency has been the revitalization of Old Sacramento. Suddenly, the colorful history of a city that was exploded into fame by the nation's most exciting event, was brought back to life from the long-forgotten past. In all, more than sixty decaying buildings were restored or reconstructed. It was the rebirth of the city's heritage.

Most of the tremendous accomplishment has been by private citizens, private businesses. Of the $300-million cost for turning an ugly frog into a princely estate, 85% has been private capital. The rest has been seed money from Federal grants given to clean out the nation's slums, and a small amount of City funds.

This turnaround of 65 blocks from blight to beauty represents the finest example in the nation, perhaps, of how redevelopment can erase decay and neglect and create charm.

It is inevitable that the Present will become the Past. So it is worthwhile to note that in history books of the Future, the remaking of historic Sacramento will be one of the most exciting chapters.

THE CHARM OF YESTERDAY

The streets of Sacramento comprise a virtual outdoor museum of Victorian homes. Some show the opulence that was the hallmark of success for men who became wealthy beyond their wildest dreams in the days that followed the Rush of Forty-Nine. Some, more modest, still preserve the fish scale shingles, the carved porch trim, the ornately turned posts and fanciful spindlework that gave pride in ownership in the 1870's.

They fan out in endless profusion for 20 blocks in any direction, from Old Town, once the heart of the city. A walking tour of almost any residential street in the area between 7th and 16th, from E to I Streets, will give an idea of the city's priceless architectural heritage. Some relics are victims of neglect, and many of the finest homes have been levelled by the wrecker's ball and replaced by advancing commercial buildings. But there are a surprising number of survivors.

The homes' early residents are long since gone. But they've left behind reminders of happy days when children ran up fancy winding staircases and slid down polished mahogany bannisters . . . when a home in a new land meant a feeling of permanence . . . when young wives planted camellia bushes that eventually grew to second story bay windows.

Few towns in the West are as well blessed with well-preserved reminders of the architectural past. . .

740 O Street...The Heilbron home was designed in 1881 by architect Nathaniel Goodell, who also built the Gallatin home, the future Governor's Mansion. Goodell recognized that the German taste of the Heilbrons didn't lean toward the frilly type of building he had erected for the Gallatins. The Heilbron home is a compact, mansard roofed building, a dignified monument to the carpenter's art. It is in splendid shiny condition, as elegant as the day the Heilbrons moved in.

517 Eighth Street...Probably designed by the same architect who created the Gallatin residence (later Governor's Mansion) and the Heilbron home.

It was built in 1894 for Mrs. William Mesick, whose husband was Sutter's attorney in his many land claims.

915 Eleventh Street...The Junior League now occupies this 1878 house built for billiard manufacturer Marcus Graff and his German Bride

800 N Street...When Leland Stanford purchased this four-story Victorian in 1861 at a cost of $8,000, there were only two floors. Ten years later, because of flooding, the house was jacked up 10 feet, creating another level below; a mansard roofline was added to make another full story. When Stanford was elected Governor, Sacramento was in another of its floods, and he departed home through the parlor window, to be escorted to his inauguration in a rowboat.

1800 J Street...Rudolph Wittenbrock and his wife crossed the plains and mountains by wagon train in 1852 and got rich growing hops. They raised eight children here; the last one stayed in the family home until 1961. It has been recently restored to its original lustre by an interior decorator firm; they encourage visitors during regular business hours,

1100 E Street...In 1894, Peter Sullivan, a foreman for the Southern Pacific, had this home built. It is a classic of Victorian style, with carvings and scrolls and ornamental window frames.

2508 F. Street...Though it looks like a cottage from the front, this 1893 residence of John Kost is quite commodious. Once it overlooked vast fields of asparagus.

1329 H Street . . . Built in 1878 at a cost of $5,000 for Hugh Duffy, an employee of Owen Casey Soda Co.

917 G Street . . . This small, neat two-story house, one of the city's few brick homes, was built in 1860 for Anthony Egl, a Hungarian who came to town in 1855 and started a wholesale dried fruit business. An innovative touch was a kitchen separate from the house, to keep the heat of cooking from adding to the normal summer heat.

1704 O Street . . . In time, Sacramentans accepted the inevitability of occasional flooding, and built a practical house (much in evidence all over town), with a second story porch and an "extra" floor below. Originally the lower level was used to store goods that wouldn't suffer from dousing. Because of 8-foot ceilings (in times when 10-foot was standard), the ground floor was considered a cellar. Today these lower levels have become part of the living quarters.

917 H Street...A grand house in Victorian Stick style, the scene of lavish parties and festive balls. Servants occupied the third floor. Llewellyn Williams, a cattle rancher, sold it after six years to a flour mill executive for $30,000 in gold. Later it became a funeral home, then headquarters for the University Club. It now rings, once again, with the sounds of hospitality, as a fine restaurant.

1931 T Street...When Fred Mason had this house built just before the turn of the century he owned a haberdashery and a steam laundry. The Masons were at the top of the social ladder, and their elegant home was in the exclusive neighborhood of town. More recently, the house has achieved fame as a setting for a Perry Mason television show.

RETURN TO SPLENDOR

When the State Capitol was completed a century or so ago, it was an edifice unrivaled for grandeur in California. Majestically it rose out of a rude and unadorned landscape, in a city that had started life as a rough-and-ready gateway to gold in 1849. Within the decade, though, Sacramento was a different story. It was an ambitious town, a steamboat port with a population of 12,000. And winning the designation of state capital had been a victory. Now legislators were looking forward to settling down in a permanent home.

Construction started in 1860.   For the next fourteen years, work proceeded in fits and starts, subject to an assortment of delays — political wrangling, shortage of materials, Sacramento's everlasting winter floods, and worst of all, from shortage of funds. Whenever money ran out, work stopped, sometimes for months at a time.   In the interim the architect went slowly insane from the strain of it (he was committed to Stockton State Hospital and died there) and never saw his project finished.

At last, in 1874, there stood the Capitol in all its glory, with its copper dome, its stately colonnades, statues, and an interior that was the opulent reflection of the current fascination with exuberant Victorian design.

But it wasn't long before the handsome structure began to show signs of growing tight at the seams. California was growing and Sacramento was expanding at a phenomenal rate, for by then the rest of the country was only a railroad ticket away.

And as the need for space become pressing, ever so gradually the spacious interior was cut up into offices. Among the first to go were the handsome carved staircases, which were sold in piece lots (some of that rare black walnut wood went into fireplaces). False ceilings were added to make mezzanine office space. (There went the coffered ceilings!)

Meanwhile, the fondness for flamboyant Victorian design had passed, lavish embellishment was passe. And so all those handsome curlicues and hand-painted murals were swabbed over with one shade of paint — institutional green.

But by 1972, a century of use was beginning to tell on the old Capitol. Paint peeled, mortar crumbled. Even the cast iron decorations were only held in place by layers of paint; the bolts had long since deteriorated. A major earthquake would have demolished the building.

Major surgery was in order. The Capitol was closed down and wouldn't be seen again by the public for six years. The entire interior was gutted, and reconstruction began from the ground up.

Rather than just put it back into sound structural shape, it was elegantly rebuilt to reflect an era when the Sacramento River was alive with steamboats and the Governor could get by with a staff of four. The ambitious project was the largest restoration in U.S. history.

It wasn't easy. Some of the original architectural drawings, for some reason, had been stored in San Francisco and had burned in the 1906 earthquake-fire. Old photographs often gave good clues. But no clues on color. What was under those layers of paint? The problem was solved by using a xenon light to remove the paint in layers -- revealing the original colors as well as ghost images of the earlier decoration.

Another special problem was the original marble mosaic on the second floor corridors. How could it be saved when the building was gutted? First the floor was photographed from above to retain an exact record, then 36-inch squares were cut out with a saw, attached to a board, and lifted out. Each of the 600,000 pieces of mosaic was cleaned, polished, grouted and glued on kraft paper. The squares were packed in boxes and reinstalled in sheets.

There were bits of luck. Fragments of friezes and medallions were found thrown away in unused spaces and under the flooring. They became patterns for artisans. A fancy newel post, carved with the head of a bear, was found in a church down the street. Woodcarvers made 34 more from that model.

Perhaps the building's most stunning feature is the exquisitely restored rotunda dome. It is painted in muted pastels, trimmed with plaster designs, gold trim and tiny lights. It is a luxurious, perhaps even ostentatious, tribute to the past.

The first floor now contains several museum rooms — historically accurate recreations of offices occupied at the turn of the century, complete with fine antique desks, bookcases and leather chairs. One is the office of Governor Pardee as it looked the day after the San Francisco earthquake. (A whimsical touch was left by the artist, who painted a medfly on the ceiling as his signature.)

Others are offices of Secretary of State, Attorney General and Treasurer as they looked in 1906.

One room, the State Library, is a fine place to browse through historic books and photo albums of the restoration project.

Free guided tours are offered daily, every hour on the hour, and visitors are also free to prowl about on their own, peeking in on the Senate and Assembly chambers, meandering through the acres of wooded park, or sitting through an orientation film on the history and restoration of the building.

It is an elegantly rebuilt statehouse. But it is more than that. It is California as it once was. And still worth cherishing.

SACRAMENTO TODAY
WHAT TO DO – WHAT TO SEE

SUTTER'S FORT, at 2701 L Street. Although the Forty-Niners did away with almost everything Sutter had created, it's all been put together again, the way it was when this was the only civilized spot of inland California.

The fort that Sutter built was remarkably complete, with all the industries needed to support life in the 19th century. In rooms surrounding the courtyard, there are carpenter, cooper and blacksmith shops, a tannery, guest quarters, the guards' quarters, a prison, and the office where Captain Sutter received Marshall the day he rode in with such excitement to tell of his gold discovery.

Audio wands re-enact some of the dramas that once took place in the old fort. It was here that weary travelers found rest, where the exhausted members of the Donner Party straggled in to recuperate from their ordeal in the Sierra snows, and where John Fremont came to consult with Sutter on the Bear Flag Rebellion.

A more recent visitor was the Queen of England, who visited the reconstructed fort in 1983.

On occasion, the events of 1846 are re-enacted with Living History Days, when artisans dressed in the dress of that day perform the chores of the blacksmith, the cooper, carpenter, spinner and weaver, and perform militia drills in the courtyard. Although these events only occur a half-dozen times a year, they are colorful and fascinating.

Sutter's Fort is open 10 to 5, seven days a week (except Christmas, Thanksgiving, and New Year's Day).

THUNDERBIRD
Sacred Bearer of
Unlimited Happiness

INDIAN MUSEUM is just around the corner from the entrance to Sutter's Fort. Archaeologists have found artifacts belonging to more than a hundred different tribes that lived in California. Many of these artifacts are on display among the Museum's exhibits, which include pottery, featherwork, dress, jewelry, and an excellent basket collection.

SUTTER'S FORT
from J. M. Letts' "California Illustrated" New York, 1852.

Living History Days in Sutter's Fort

CROCKER ART GALLERY was begun by Mrs. E. B. Crocker, wife of the attorney/brother of railroad magnate Charles Crocker, after she returned from a trip to Europe where she collected many fine paintings and art objects. It's been greatly enlarged since then.

The Crocker is the oldest art gallery/museum west of the Mississippi, and many of its paintings are classics of the Old West, including the famous "Sunday Morning in the Mines." The beautiful old home is an architectural art object in itself. There's a gift shop on the lower level. And the museum often features afternoon concerts, lectures, films and other cultural events. Location: 216 O Street.

300 O Street...Originally owned by B.F. Hastings, this three-story brick house was built in 1853. When Judge Edwin Crocker, attorney to the Big Four, was appointed a Supreme Court Justice by Governor Stanford, the Crockers bought it and did some remodeling. The art gallery was added in 1873 following a trip to Europe.

CHURCH OF THE BLESSED SACRAMENT on 11th Street, was built in 1889 under the direction of Bishop Patrick Manogue, who built St. Mary's in the Mountains at Virginia City and became the friend to the miners. The Diocese was in Grass Valley until the persuasive Bishop Manogue went to Rome and petitioned for its transfer to Sacramento. The architectural design came from Paris; the stained glass from Innsbruck, Austria (at least, most of it). Particularly notable is the huge painting given to the cathedral by Mrs. Leland Stanford in thanks for special attention given to her young son by monks in Italy when he was taken ill there.

GOVERNOR'S MANSION. It was once the home of the Gallatins, who made their money in hardware. They spared nothing in having the finest, particularly in the field Gallatin knew best (and could get wholesale), hardware. It is a grand example of architectural gingerbread in the Victorian style. After the turn of the century when Victorian houses were no longer in style, governors occasionally complained about the small rooms, the high ceilings, the old-fashioned style. But Earl Warren, who lived there longest, declared he liked it fine and found good exercise in running up and down the flights of stairs. The Edmund Browns thought it had a lot of charm. And by then Victorian style was back in vogue again. However, the Reagans were accustomed to Southern California "open" style of architecture, and so the old mansion was abandoned as the official Governor's residence. It is now a historical landmark. Tours are conducted daily, between 10 a.m. and 4:30 p.m., every half hour.

OLD SACRAMENTO is now a State Historical Park, and some of the old structures have been restored to their original use. One of the notable is the B. F. Hastings Building at Second and J, which once housed a bank and the Wells Fargo express office. Another tenant was the State Supreme Court, which moved into the second floor in 1855 and held sessions there for two years. The upstairs Court and adjoining offices look today much as they did when justice was meted out in tumultuous gold rush times.

Other exhibits in the Hastings Building tell the story of the early telegraph, stage lines, the postal service, and the Pony Express, for it was in front of the Hastings Building that the first rider arrived from Missouri with mail for California.

The Big Four Building, named for the Big Four of western railroading—Stanford, Hopkins, Huntington & Crocker—now houses the Huntington-Hopkins Hardware store, as it did in the 1880s. The second floor is the recreation of the Central Pacific's board room. Hours 10 am to 5 pm. (Free admission)

Another ancient building, the Firehouse, was erected in 1853. It was said that the horses were so well trained that when the alarm rang they tromped to the front on their own, ready to be hitched. The building, oldest firehouse in Sacramento, was restored in 1961, and was the cornerstone for the "preservation for use" theme of the entire Old Sacramento project.

DISCOVERY MUSEUM. Located at Front and I Streets, it's a recreation of the first City Hall and Waterworks Building of 1854, which stood on the site.

The museum chronicles local and national events, from the Gold Rush and Pony Express to the sweeping changes in California agriculture during the past century. It is an archives and museum, a look at life in another time, and a research center.

Included among its exhibits will be a special collection of historic printing equipment and newspapers, and letters dating back to Sacramento's beginnings.

TOWE FORD MUSEUM, the world's most comprehensive collection of antique Fords, has on display every model car produced by Ford between 1903 and 1953, and a few beyond that.

Henry Ford never set out to make glamour cars for the rich and famous. His forte was "the car for the common man."

The museum is a repository for every year of Model T and Model A, including the sporty 1929 Model A roadster (original price $450!) and a handsome 1930 wooden-body station wagon. But there are some uncommonly jazzy models too. A real beauty is the elegant 1935 V8 Phaeton cloth top. Another stunner is the 1957 Skyliner with a retractable hard top that folds up to fit into the trunk. All cars are beautifully restored or in good original condition.

Located at 2200 Front Street, it is just a short distance south from Old Sacramento. (Front Street can be reached via 2nd Street underpass from Old Sacramento, or via O Street from Crocker Art Gallery.)

JAZZ FESTIVAL. Once a year, on the Memorial Day weekend, Old Sacramento turns into a New Orleans of the North, when the town goes wild over Dixieland jazz. Groups arrive from all over the country as well as such bastions of American jazz as Amsterdam, Holland. Then the aging buildings of Old Sacramento literally rock to the beat as hundreds of bands blow their horns, and fans go wild with clapping and stomping.

THE RAILROAD MUSEUM

Near the old railroad tracks on J Street in Old Sacramento stands the riverfront store where the mighty Central Pacific had its beginnings. Once this modest building was the headquarters office for the four small-town merchants who undertook the greatest achievement of 19th century America.

A visit to this hardware store should be the prelude to seeing another epic achievement — the construction of the California State Railroad Museum, one of the world's largest and finest collections of railroad memorabilia. This is no ordinary museum. It's a production Walt Disney would be proud of.

It's a museum where you are encompassed by the sights and sounds and overwhelming sensations of railroading. An array of images flashed on a hundred ingeniously designed projection cubes is accompanied by the sound of a lonely whistle blowing in the night, the chugging of a locomotive pulling up a long grade, a clanging signal.

A 12-minute film tells graphically the story of the events of 1850-1869, events that brought to completion the nation's first transcontinental railroad. When the film ends, you can walk right into the scene you've just viewed — see the locomotive on the track, watch the patient Chinese laborers chiseling through ice and snow and solid granite in the bitterly cold Sierra winter. It's the only walk-in diorama ever attempted in a railroad museum. Its realism is startling.

But it's only the prelude for a vast complex of similar scenes that make the History Building seem more like a slice-of-life than a museum.

Everywhere in the multi-level building there are vintage locomotives and passenger cars and freight cars, all in realistic settings that depict what railroads meant to the West. They tell of migrations of settlers, the architecture of the depot, the affluence of private cars, the excitement of trains that brought the circus to town, the luxury of the streamliners, and of the refrigerated cars that turned California into an agricultural state, able to send fresh vegetables to the rest of the country. And the trains, resting on authentic rails, are totally functional. They could be placed directly into service on tracks outside the building that link Sacramento with the rest of America.

Some of the rolling stock was donated by railroad companies, but much of it resulted from the foresight of the Pacific Coast Chapter of the Railway & Locomotive Historical Society, which started collecting the pieces, large and small, twenty years ago.

The ambitious History Building project is the third phase of the museum complex. The first phase was the rebuilding of the Central Pacific Railroad station on the original site where the first transcontinental railroad began in 1863. The station is a dead ringer for the original one where so many eager passengers indulged in the sensation of the 1860s, 70s, and 80s — a trip on the train.

There are other big railroad museums, but this one gets all awards for being the best interpretive museum in the world. It's authentic enough to satisfy the most discerning railroad buff, yet, enticing enough for the casual visitor who has never been near a train.

The Historic California Delta

The California Delta is a backwater region that looks like nothing else in the state: old towns with board sidewalks, the remains of river landings built for steamboats that will not come again, acres and acres of agricultural fields lying below sea level, and a thousand navigable miles of rivers and sloughs, crossed by no less than 70 bridges and five tiny ferries.

On a road map, the region appears rather small, bounded roughly by the main cities of Sacramento and Stockton, Antioch and Rio Vista. But a glance at a nautical chart reveals the true intricate vastness of this interlocking system of waterways, formed when three major rivers tumble togther with a score of streams into a sort of bayou, eventually to meld with San Francisco Bay.

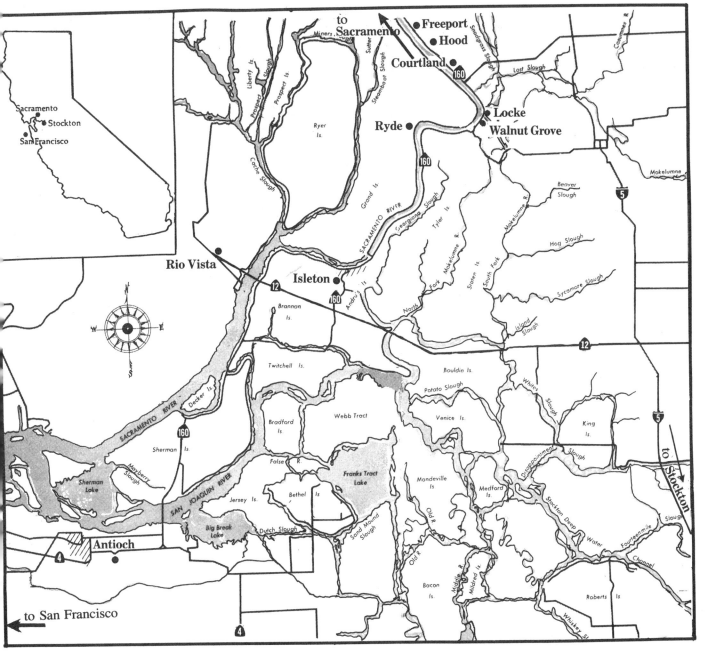

In far earlier times, when Spanish explorers discovered the delta, it was a swampy wilderness

This was also the setting when Captain Sutter, in 1839, made his way through the convoluted waterways to claim the land so generously granted him by Mexico's governor — land no one else wanted because it was a swamp.

For the next two years, Sutter had only a four-oared boat to travel the Delta. But when he purchased Fort Ross in 1841, he acquired a schooner, and for several years it was the only vessel to ply Delta waters. Finding knowledgeable crewmen was another matter.

Incompetent pilots would enter the network of sloughs and row about for days before they were extricated. Some perished in the tules and were never found.

As late as 1847, according to one contemporary account, "from the Stanislaus river to Marsh's Landing (now Antioch), not a house did we pass, nor did we even see an Indian."

But the discovery of gold at Coloma in 1848 changed the waterways forever, turning them into arteries of commerce.

In the early days of the Gold Rush, when prospectors swarmed to the foothills, the Delta was virtually the only access to inland California. Men afflicted with gold fever needed transportation to the diggings. Sacramento merchants, who suddenly found a brisk trade going in picks and shovels, needed supplies.

Soon, steamers were chugging up and down the river, as many as 28 in 1849 to Sacramento, somewhat less to Stockton. The ship *Senator* established regular passenger service, charging $30 for passage. And within a few years, some of America's finest steamboats were making regular runs through the Delta waters.

But the gold fields did not bring prosperity to all. And inevitably the rich peat soil along the river banks came to the notice of men disenchanted with toiling in the mines.

Most settlers wanted only to make gardens to grow food to fill their own bellies. But periodic floods would flush their carrot crops and chicken coops out to sea. So the gardeners built what they called "shoestring levees" on the tops of mounds of dirt that had already accumulated. The crude levees deflected the floodwater, held back the seawater, and kept the garden soil in place.

They built the first levees with shovels. But in 1869, when the transcontinental railroad was finished and hundreds of Chinese laborers were released, they were hired at $1 a day to build bigger levees. For the Chinese, this was an ancient trade, one they knew well. They were innovative, and when mules sank up to their knees in mud, the levee builders made tiny snowshoes for them to re-distribute the weight.

The famous *Delta King* — steaming through the Delta.

The results of the first farming efforts were almost miraculous. Reports cited cabbages weighing 53 pounds a head and potatoes measuring 33 inches in circumference.

In no time at all, new farms on new islands were being enclosed and shored up by levees. Farmers settled in and began growing fruits and vegetables with such success that they were supplying the tables of the world.

Those were the glory days of the Delta. Handsome steamboats touched at 65 different landings, bringing supplies, picking up cargoes of produce, transporting passengers on luxurious runs between Sacramento and San Francisco.

One of the steamboats, the *Delta Queen,* (now of Mississippi River fame), hosted pleasure cruises for 15 years. What a beauty she was: a four-tiered wedding cake with hand rails of polished teakwood, lounges adorned with Tiffany stained glass windows, a dining room with a floor of Siamese ironbark and glistening crystal chandeliers.

But the advent of the automobile made river traffic obsolete. By the 1930s, river shipping had become virtually non-existent.

Today the Delta floats an assortment of recreational watercraft — rowboats, yachts, sailboats, speedy jets pulling waterskiers, sleek new houseboats.

Still, with all its popularity, the Delta never seems crowded. Within its winding channels are miles of offshoot streams to explore and secluded havens for anchoring in estuaries bearing such colorful names as Potato Slough, Whiskey Slough, Five Fingers, and Hog Island.

But the Delta is more than a boater's world. Along miles and miles of levee roads and the secondary farm roads that sprout from them, are such sleepy old towns (once steamboat landings) as Isleton, Courtland, Hood, Locke, Walnut Grove, and Ryde. They linger on from the past, with a kind of dusty charm and the after-flavor of riverboating days clinging to them.

The drawbridge at Freeport yawns open to let the *Delta King* pass.

LOCKE

One of the most colorful of the Delta's hamlets is Locke, the West's only surviving all-Chinese town, its rickety, two-story, porticoed, clapboard buildings sandwiched together on two narrow streets.

Although it has the appearance of Gold Rush days, it was actually built in 1912 by the Chinese, using land of their benefactor, George Locke. (Orientals were then forbidden to own land.) The deal was sealed with the customary Delta "notarization" – a handshake – and everyone chipped in some money toward the development of six two-story houses costing $1,200 each. They also built a hotel, restaurants, flour mill, slaughterhouse, bakery, and a Chinese language school.

Locke's fragile wooden buildings have been spared the fires that racked other Delta settlements because of the *bok bok* man – a night watchman who made his rounds from 6 p.m. until dawn. After each round he struck the "bok-bok," a hollow wooden block (used as a musical instrument) to reassure the residents that all was well.

Perhaps Locke's greatest fame was as a gambling town. In prime days, there were five gambling houses in Locke (one survives today as a gambling museum). When first opened, they catered exclusively to the Chinese, and women were not allowed, though later Filipino farm workers without family became patrons, and Japanese were welcome. Eventually Caucasians found their way to the tables. Occasional raids by the law were taken lightly, and the halls quickly reopened. But in 1951 they closed forever.

Today fewer than a hundred souls live in Locke, most of them elderly men and all trying desperately for privacy. Along the creaking boardwalk are the false-front Republic Cafe building, the Star Theater, an art gallery, and Locke's most famous establishment, the legendary saloon-steakhouse irreverently known as Al-the-Wop's.

———————————————————

WALNUT GROVE

Only a mile downriver from Locke is another town that once held a high population of Chinese. Its Chinese sector was a dark, winding ground warren seldom penetrated by Caucasians. In asparagus-picking season, it had an abnormally high population of thousands. But the old settlement was destroyed by fire. Most of its residents picked up what remained of their belongings and established the Locke community.

Walnut Grove was founded in 1851 by John Sharp, who recognized a good location when he saw it – the spot where Georgiana Slough met the Sacramento River. Since travelers found difficulty crossing the river at that point, Sharp set up a successful ferry service.

Sharp was nothing if not ambitious. His list of accomplishments over the next 30 years included raising eight children, managing a dairy farm of 360 acres, operating the ferry, a hotel, blacksmith shop, serving as postmaster, and constructing a steamboat landing.

When he died at age 57, his widow sold his interests to Agnes Brown, whose son was destined for fame as founder of Bank of Alex Brown.

Before opening the bank, Brown loaned money to farmers from his own pocket, and leased land to the Japanese in an agreement secured by only a handshake.

Walnut Grove exists on both sides of the river. The west bank has the comfortable residential community with some fine old houses. The east bank is more colorful, its dusty old streets lined with buildings that still hold the faint lettering of long-past times.

COURTLAND

A few miles upriver from Locke and Walnut Grove, the hamlet of Courtland perches precariously on a levee bank, the back of its buildings propped on stilts.

Only a handful of buildings remain in this "pear capital of the Delta," among them the still-handsome, neo-classical Bank of Courtland, looking for all the world like a Greek temple. Once the heartbeat of the Delta's post-World War I boom, the bank now stands in lonely dignity, unoccupied. Like the rest of the Delta's then-thriving businesses, it was done in by the twin blows of the Depression and a dwindling river traffic.

> *Levi Painter, who founded a landing near Courtland in 1852 (known as Paintersville) instigated a most unusual institution known as his Post Hole Bank.*
>
> *Well known to be an honest man, he was often asked by local people to hold their gold and coins in safekeeping when they had to leave temporarily. Fearing that he might be robbed, Painter devised a banking system of his own. He started building a fence, working only at night, and buried the funds under certain memorized fence posts.*

Nearby Hood, a modest village of a few shops, lives on mainly as a shipping point for local Bartlett pears being sent to far-flung markets.

But in the nearby pear orchards, a large number of handsome Victorian farm houses can be seen. Most handsome of the lot is Rosebud Farm (now on the national register of historic buildings), slightly north of Hood.

FREEPORT

After the West's first railroad was built to Folsom, Sacramento elected to place a levy on every passenger and pound of freight that left the river to connect with the trains. The Railroad objected to this action, and pulled out of Sacramento to establish a new port down the river which would be free. This is how the town of Freeport got its name.

Photo courtesy of A.J. Bump's of Freeport

Freeport's first building was a General Store established in 1863 by A.J. Bump, whose first customers were passers-by on the Sacramento road. Since the men leaned more to liquid refreshment than groceries, his profit derived mainly from wet goods, plus the games of chance he promoted. The house never lost at these games, and Bump carried his profits in a little velvet bag in his fat hip pocket.

Among the greatest architectural treasures of the Delta is River Mansion on Grand Island. Built in the 1920s by Louis Myers, it is the residue of days when asparagus barons and pear kings built opulent homes, never dreaming that agricultural prosperity could end.

Complete with ballroom, theater and bowling alley, the mansion was built as the result of rivalry between Mrs. Myers and Mrs. William Smith, who built "The Castle."

No expense was spared. European craftsmen were called in. A curving staircase rose from a grand entrance hall. The living room featured a raised stage at one end for private recitals. The kitchen was immense, the dining room paneled in dark oak. The four stories overlooked a court-yard enclosed on three sides to protect it from prevailing winds.

Guests arriving at the estate could tie up then – as now – at a 50-foot pier on Steamboat Slough.

But Myers held no parties there; he died before it was finished. He made a serious miscalculation turning his field crops into orchards – which had to wait ten years to be harvested. He had borrowed heavily and lived beyond his means, and the bank foreclosed. It was perhaps little comfort to his widow that the bank also foreclosed on the Smith estate.

Today the four-story mansion sits serenely along a cypress-lined circular drive, its entrance framed by 30-foot Corinthian columns. Over the years its rooms have rung with the merry laughter of lavish parties that entertained such notables as Ronald Reagan, Jean Harlow, and Governor Jerry Brown.

Now privately owned and renovated, it's the scene of Sunday brunches.

* ———————————————————————— *

RYDE

Even at its peak, this hamlet on Grand Island could boast little more than a few homes, a post office and a landing. Today it lives mostly in the memory of more vivid times, when its hotel was a noted speakeasy.

Riverboats made regular stops at the hotel's pier, and guests eagerly sought accommodations in its 51 rooms and six private dining rooms. The main dining room gleamed with elegance and respectability, but the basement was a different story. It was a speakeasy filled with slot machines and a long bar.

A secret tunnel ran from the basement's rest-rooms to a building 150 feet away. The small building housed the still which produced the gin and whiskey. The illegal liquor was then carried through the tunnel to the speakeasy, and then to the hotel's private dining rooms or aboard the steamers docked at the pier.

One touring U.S. president with teetotaler leanings little knew he was making a campaign speech one floor above the bootlegger's cache.

Law enforcement officers made four raids on the hotel, and finally discovered the secret tunnel and sealed it shut.

Today the hotel, renamed the Grand Island Hotel, is a versatile nightspot, in the same 1920s style as its more flamboyant days.

ISLETON

Isleton's Chinatown, 1930.

Things have not always gone well for this town on Andrus Island. Early farmers planted vegetables, peach and apricot trees, but their crops were heavily damaged when mining chemicals and debris from Sierra foothill gold mines washed down into the Sacramento River.

Floods devastated the community on several occasions. And fires have raked the Chinese quarters several times.

Still, it has become a prosperous center for Bartlett pear orchards and once claimed to be the "Asparagus Capital of the World."

At one time Isleton had, in addition to its large Chinese population, a thriving Japantown which attracted such exotic performers as *Sumo* wrestlers and *Kabuki* theater groups.

Today, Isleton is more famous for being ensconced in prime fishing waters.

RIO VISTA

There have been two Rio Vistas. The first was built on land bought for 15¢ an acre from Sutter's good friend, John Bidwell.

Things were going well in the new settlement; a 75-foot wharf brought river commerce, a post office was installed. But in January 1862 disaster struck. Rushing flood waters washed away the entire town.

The survivors appealed to two local ranchers to build a new town on their land, and the new town prospered — in part because it attracted the world's largest asparagus cannery.

But there was more. For years, Rio Vista was the only Delta port-of-call for the packet ships. All of the region's trade funnelled there.

The Rio Vista drawbridge is one of the busiest in the Delta. But far more interesting is the tiny ferry called The Real McCoy, which operates off Highway 84 just north of Rio Vista, crossing Cache Slough to Ryer Island.

It runs 24 hours a day, carries six cars. The voyage is only 400 yards long, to a levee on Ryer Island where Highway 220 leads to Ryde. Halfway there, there's another tiny ferry, the J-Mack, this one cable-operated. Both can be crossed in one short circle trip — and they are free.

ANTIOCH

Considered by some (especially Antioch residents) to be the "Gateway to the Delta," the town has changed considerably since the 1884 *Pacific Tourist* magazine called it "a pleasant village of 300 with a sprightly weekly paper."

Antioch's most famous feature for years was a lift-span bridge considered the largest highway bridge in the West (before the Bay and Golden Gate bridges). When large ships passed, the middle section would rise 135 feet above the water to allow entry to the Deepwater Channel.

Still, there were collisions. And in September 1970 the freighter "SS Washington Bear" brushed the bridge on its way through, so that the lift span tower was tilted three feet to the east, jamming the span in the "up" position and trapping the bridge operator for 18 hours in his control cabin high above the river. The bridge was closed for four months.

It has since been replaced by a new high-rise bridge 250 feet downtream.

* ———————————————————————————— *

STOCKTON

Stockton's busy waterfront in the 1870s.

The Gold Rush created almost as much havoc in Stockton as Sacramento. With thousands of adventurers needing transportation to the interior, the few sailing vessels available were totally inadequate and too slow. Steam was, thus far, unheard of.

So it was small wonder that when the first steamer (named the *John Sutter*) steamed up Stockton channel, streamers flying, the large and excited crowd that had formed on the bank sent up cheer after cheer – for the boat and for her gallant captain.

According to a contemporary account, "The event was celebrated by a general indulgence in conviviality by citizenry and crew; and if any of the party walked a little crooked, there were no zealous police taking them in tow."

The *Sutter* was the first of many steamers, built in quick succession.

Alas, a short life was the common fate of steamers in those days.

The *Sutter*, withdrawn from the Stockton run in favor of Sacramento, blew up – a total wreck – never to be rebuilt.

The *El Dorado*, replacing the *Sutter* on the Stockton run, couldn't meet the demand so another, the *Sagamore*, was added. She had just started up the San Joaquin, crowded with passengers, when her boilers exploded. Loss of life: 50 persons. Fault: The engineer.

That same evening the *Mariposa* was run into by the *West Point* in Suisun Bay and sank to water level. Passengers were transferred to the nearby *El Dorado*; which generously lowered fares from $20 per person to $18.

But risky as steamer travel may have been, it was a start. The steamers and the paddlewheelers of the Delta were followed by giant freighters. And when the world of pleasure boats discovered the South Delta waters, Stockton took an early lead by putting in a Municipal Guest Dock right near the heart of the city.

THE EASYGOING LIFE OF THE DELTA

The Delta is not for those in a hurry. The mood here is one of suspended time, subtle scenery changes, curious exploration, lazy fishing. Those who love it most refer to themselves, in half-joking pride, as "river rats."

An hour's drive east of San Francisco, its waterways make it one of the most versatile recreation areas in California, visited by millions each year.

One popular area is Brannan Island State Recreation Area, formed in 1929 when Army Engineers dredged the Sacramento River channel and needed some place to dump the silt.

Another recreation area that draws visitors is Frank's Tract, a large but shallow lake that was once a prosperous ranch. A break in the levee in 1938 inundated the island, forming the lake in the process. It is known as a "hot spot" by anglers, who come for the catfish and striped bass.

Next to Frank's, Bethel Island is a sort of headquarters for those who find their pleasure in boating, fishing, waterskiing. Its kickback attitude has drawn a population of 3,000, though weekends will see 10,000.

Fishing is an all-year activity on the Delta, but spring and fall are the peak seasons for one of the Delta's most sought-after game fish, the striped bass. Salmon and steelhead pass through on their fall migration up the Sacramento River. And although it's unusual, the sturgeon caught during the winter months may run to 1300 pounds. Fightingest fish in the Delta is the largemouth bass. Bluegill and other panfish are routinely taken. But the most dependable fishing is for catfish, which takes the bait almost any time.

The Delta has also achieved international fame for its crayfish, with enormous catches being shipped to Sweden, where this is a prized delicacy.

Many people consider houseboating the ideal way to explore the low-key Delta. These slow-moving, floating apartments set a properly pokey pace for lazy days of sunning, swimming, fishing, trapping crayfish, and watching the passing parade of speedboats, skiers, and sailboats.

The levees run every which way and are a vital part of the Delta. For those who find no calling to the boater's world, the levee roads provide wonderful access to the Delta world. Highway 160 snakes from bank to bank for 45 miles. By following that road and the secondary farm roads, the motorist gets some sense of the Delta's spell. The roads are usually traffic-free and great for driving, biking, or a sunny morning stroll.

The Delta may be California's most undiscovered recreational asset. Its austere marshland beauty has been largely overlooked by travelers who flock to the state's more flamboyant landscapes.

But those who like the idea of falling asleep to the sound of lapping water, crickets in the foliage, birds by the thousands and bass jumping to catch night insects, believe they've found it all — and more — in the California Delta.